The Abingdon Preaching Annual 2020

D1569954

The Abingdon
Preaching
Annual

2020

Planning Sermons and Services
for Fifty-Two Sundays

Tanya Linn Bennett, General Editor

Abingdon Press

Nashville

THE ABINGDON PREACHING ANNUAL 2020:
PLANNING SERMONS AND SERVICES FOR FIFTY-TWO SUNDAYS

Copyright © 2019 by Abingdon Press

This book is printed on acid-free paper.

ISBN 978-1-5018-8124-4

Excerpt on page 156 taken from Charley Reeb, *Say Something! Simple Ways to Make Your Sermons Matter*, copyright © 2019 by Abingdon Press. Used by permission. All rights reserved.

Excerpt on page 158 taken from Joni S. Sancken, *Words That Heal: Preaching Hope to Wounded Souls*, copyright © 2019 by Abingdon Press. Used by permission. All rights reserved.

Excerpt on page 160 taken from David B. Ward, *Practicing the Preaching Life*, copyright © 2019 by Abingdon Press. Used by permission. All rights reserved.

Excerpt on page 153 taken from Lenny Luchetti, *Preaching with Empathy: Crafting Sermons in a Callous Culture*, copyright © 2018 by Abingdon Press. Used by permission. All rights reserved.

Excerpt on page 162 taken from Paul Scott Wilson, *The Four Pages of a Sermon, Revised and Updated: A Guide to Biblical Preaching*, copyright © 2018 by Abingdon Press. Used by permission. All rights reserved.

Scripture unless otherwise noted is from the Common English Bible. Copyright © 2011 by the Common English Bible. All rights reserved. Used by permission. www.CommonEnglishBible.com.

Scripture marked NRSV is from the New Revised Standard Version Bible, copyright © 1989 National Council of the Churches of Christ in the United States of America. Used by permission. All rights reserved worldwide. http://nrsvbibles.org

Scripture marked NIV is taken from the Holy Bible, New International Version®, NIV®. Copyright © 1973, 1978, 1984, 2011 by Biblica, Inc.™ Used by permission of Zondervan. All rights reserved world-wide. www.zondervan.com The "NIV" and "New International Version" are trademarks registered in the United States Patent and Trademark Office by Biblica, Inc.™

Scripture marked KJV is from The Authorized (King James) Version. Rights in the Authorized Version in the United Kingdom are vested in the Crown. Reproduced by permission of the Crown's patentee, Cambridge University Press.

19 20 21 22 23 24 25 26 27 28—10 9 8 7 6 5 4 3 2 1
MANUFACTURED IN THE UNITED STATES OF AMERICA

Contents

🌿 = Sunday in Lent   ⚘ = Sunday of Advent

ESSAYS FOR SKILL-BUILDING

Acknowledgments

My deep thanksgiving for Abingdon editorial staff members Constance Stella, Peggy Shearon, and Laurie Perry Vaughen. I thank Constance for, first, the offer to undertake this editing project, and second, patiently guiding and supporting this fledgling editor. And deep thanksgiving, too, for the many, varied, engaged voices of those who have poured out their wisdom and words to create this volume. These prophetic congregational leaders, deacons, elders, bishops, general secretaries, artists, musicians, conspired with me to shape this resource of their lived experience and worldview, and their unique approach to delivering a word in context that might open ears and clear a cluttered, clanging world to hear new truth and hope.

—Tanya Linn Bennett, General Editor

Editor's Introduction

"Come Sunday, oh, come Sunday, that's the day. Lord, dear Lord above, God Almighty, God of love, please look down and see my people through." These words from the Duke Ellington hymn appear in the section of *The United Methodist Hymnal* titled "A New Heaven and a New Earth." In his commentary about this hymn, C. Michael Hawn quotes African American scholar William McClain: "To the Christian Sunday is, or should be, another Easter, in which God's victory in Christ over sin and death are celebrated in work, word, song, prayer, and preaching."[1]

What would it mean to the spiritual thriving of those who gather to worship on Sunday, and to our own spiritual lives, if we approached every opportunity for worship with the same eagerness and excitement as we do Easter Sunday? How do we continue to engage and pastorally address the strife, the sweetness, the challenge, the consolation, and the many cares of the beloved who gather? At this time, in this church, how do we make song, word, and ritual into a worship experience that transforms, even transfigures, our hearts and minds and actions as Christian people? It is my prayer that the thoughts, ideas, interpretations, and concepts of those who have contributed to this volume will inspire all of us in ways we have not yet imagined to make every Sunday a day when a new heaven and a new earth might emerge, crafted by the Holy Spirit in conspiration with the body of Christ.

—*Tanya Linn Bennett, General Editor*

January 5, 2020–Epiphany

Passages: Isaiah 60:1-6; Psalm 72:1-7, 10-14; Ephesians 3:1-12;
Matthew 2:1-12

Tanya Linn Bennett

Prayer

In the season of gloom, the light arrives. God, call us to stop still, standing at the side of the newborn babe, leaning in with admiration. Stunned in glory. Shocked with awe. Wide awake in knowing that nothing will ever be the same. Piercing the gloom, the light arrives. Epiphany. Thanks be to God.

Preaching Theme

"Arise! Shine! Your light has come;
the Lord's glory has shone upon you.
Though darkness covers the earth
and gloom the nations,
the Lord will shine upon you."

These words of great hope and mighty blessing in Isaiah 60:1-2 fall upon the people of Israel in a time of restoration. Returning as exiles from Babylon to Jerusalem, these sixth-century BCE Israelites find their holy city lying in ruins. While exiled, the writer of Isaiah 3 has extolled the people to be repentant, to abandon their unrighteous ways. And now these outrageous words: "Arise! Shine! Your light has come; the LORD's glory has shone upon you." Imperative language to call a people back to, out of, and to rebuild a nation. To those of us who would hope that rebuilding a nation would mean tearing down the walls, redistributing wealth and power in a more equitable way, and reconsidering the ways in which we organize our society, the challenge of this chapter in Isaiah is that it goes on to describe a restoration of the establishment as it was before the exile, with the same hierarchical indicators. Absolute submission to this imperial structure will be necessary for those who wish to experience the possibilities of redemption and forgiveness God offers.

So, what we might do as preachers of this powerful text is to both reveal the faults of the text in terms of creating a just society, but also to explore the hopefulness of this text for those of us living in nations violence-torn, politically fractured, and one-percentivized. What the Bible proves to us is that society structured imperially, with power focused in a small elite, does not work to the common good, which is God's vision for creation. As we consider this text in the season following Advent, centralizing the notion of Jesus, a brand-new thing birthed by Mary and the Spirit offers a critical contrast to this imperial theme in a deeper exploration of this Isaiah text.

Secondary Preaching Theme

It might be surprising to some, but I find Herod a rather pathetic character in this passage from Matthew. In the midst of the great joy of the arrival of Emmanuel, God with Us, I imagine Herod holing up in his castle, wringing his hands, worried and fearful—"troubled," as our text says. Using his kingly authority, he summons the astrologists to his office to demand that they report back to him after following the Great Star to the side of the newborn king—of course, so that he also could "honor" the newborn king of the Jews. While the three wise ones journey on, following the bright light to the holy baby's crib, Herod remains behind, beholden to these strangers to do his bidding. The astrologists look upon the radiant face of the newborn king, bestow their symbolic gifts, and go home by another route, having been "warned in a dream" not to return to King Herod.

What happens to Herod? Does Herod ever look up to see the bright star, to imagine a new life in a new time? Or do his fear and worry keep him trapped in his great mansion, alone and troubled? How many of us find ourselves trapped in this season of Epiphany, scared and alone, rather than looking up and out to see what is around us? In the quiet dim that follows the great pageant of Christmas, would we take a moment to settle our troubled hearts and reach out for the newborn king, Emmanuel, God with Us, and walk in the great light that God has set in the stars to light our path?

Epiphany Communion Setting

Every January 6, in the midst of the Epiphany celebration, Ethiopian Christians celebrate the baptism of Christ, gathering along the shores of the Jordan River. Dressed in white gowns, they toss themselves into the gently flowing water of the Jordan. They cheer and sing and splash with joy at the reminder of who and whose they are. This communion liturgy was inspired by my witness of this faithful gathering in 2012.

Invitation: *All are invited to touch the waters of baptism and eat and drink of the food of life. Before we come to be filled, we are emptied.*

Confession: *God of grace and mercy, we beg to be drenched in the water that makes us clean and filled with the food that makes us whole. We stutter and stagger on our way to the water and the table. Untangle our feet to walk your way, and free our tongues to shout of your joy, justice, and love.*

Passing of the Peace

Great Thanksgiving:
God is here.
God is with us.

With fingers oozing with, squishing in the
deep rich clay of the Dead Sea
the fine glassy sand of the Sea of Galilee
the silky silt of the River Jordan
God shaped us, breathed into us, and set us on the planet formed from chaos.
With faithfulness beyond measure and patience beyond deserving, God set us on our way,
and watched, and waited. When our love failed and our feet wandered, God remained,
ever and always, our Maker and our Re-maker.

Sanctus:
(*The Faith We Sing*, 2257 b)

With hands clutching, clinging, clearing
God gripped the sandy, silky clay again.
In palms rich with love and peace and hope, God shaped the One,
the One who came to set us free.
The One baptized and beloved.
We could not bear such goodness ourselves,
or share it with each other.
But with faithfulness beyond measure and patience beyond deserving,
God promises again and always that the One lives among us
And beyond us.

Memorial Acclamation—FWS 2257 c

May the heavens open here and now, pouring your love onto us and into this food.
May we be bread for the world, fed by the food made holy in your heart.
As the Spirit calls us Beloved, may we call your world Beloved.

Consecration of the Elements

Jesus offered the Passover bread to the disciples, the ones he gathered from the shoreline,
the ones who watched him still the waters, the ones who stood on the deck of the boat as
it crossed the Sea of Galilee. He blessed it, broke it, and shared it, saying, "Do this and
remember that this is what makes us one. This is what makes us whole."
He took the cup, blessed it, shared it and said, "Do this and remember God's everlasting
promise to love us into new life over and over again."
With the confidence of those who have heard the promise and remember, let us pray the
prayer that Jesus taught us.

-3

Lord's Prayer

Sharing of the Elements

Closing Words

Bathed in the baptism waters, we go forth, the beloved ones ready to love the world just as it is with all that we have been made to be.

January 12, 2020–
First Sunday after Epiphany;
Baptism of the Lord

Passages: Isaiah 42:1-9; Psalm 29; Acts 10:34-43; Matthew 3:13-17

Javier Viera

Gathering Prayer

In the primordial waters, O Lord, you brought forth all that is.
In the waters of the womb, O Lord, you fashioned us.
In the waters of baptism, O Lord, you claim us.
Stir up the waters again, O Lord, that they may once more bring forth your
glory and your intention.
As your voice spoke at Jesus's baptism, speak once more to us this day.
May your voice, strong and majestic, make clear our true identity as your beloved, and
may it unleash in us the spirit of adventure and desire to proclaim your good news of jus-
tice, mercy, and love throughout the earth. Amen.

Preaching Theme

Baptism is serious business. A National Public Radio story a few years back told of a seventy-one-year-old Frenchman who was seeking to be de-baptized.[1] The man, Rene LeBouvier, formally petitioned French church officials to annul or invalidate his baptism. He had been raised in a very religious family, and his mother dreamed that one day he might become a priest. Yet, in the 1970s, like many of his counterparts, Rene dared to explore intellectually beyond the confines of his strict Catholic, religious community, and that was the beginning of the end as far as his faith was concerned.

After years of attempting to have his name removed from church rolls and baptismal records, Mr. LeBouvier learned that this simply was not possible. He then decided to take the church to court. A magistrate found in his favor, but the church appealed. It was not possible to erase history, they argued, nor to deny that a sacred rite had taken place, vows and eternal declarations made.

Baptism is more than simply a rite of passage or a religious ceremony; it's one of life's defining, threshold-crossing moments. It's a destiny moment when, whether you chose it or not, you were declared God's beloved "and marked as Christ's own forever," as the liturgy poetically states. Nothing you can do, even renouncing your faith, can ever nullify that fact. This is why baptism is serious business.

In baptism we claim that everything changes. That's what happened at Jesus's own baptism. It was literally a "heavens opening" moment. Imagine Jesus as Matthew depicts him—curious, searching, insightful, precocious. Being spiritually adventurous, he decided to go down by the river, where so many others were flocking to hear his relative, John, preach a fiery message, and they were being baptized into a new relationship with God. There is so much we cannot know about that day and what motivated Jesus to join John and the others, but what we do know is that at the moment of his baptism, everything changed. He went down to the river that day searching, longing, open, and he came back a changed man. He discovered, or had confirmed, his true identity and the true nature of his relationship to God. The church has always claimed that in baptism the same is true for each of us.

This is why Mr. LeBouvier cannot be de-baptized. What happened to him as a child in baptism had the essence of God in it, regardless of how broken the institution that celebrated this truth might be and regardless of Mr. LeBouvier's later rejection of God's eternal declaration about him. His baptism cannot be undone because it was God's doing in the first place. The good news about our God is that God's choice to love us so fully, and to claim us eternally, cannot be undone.

Secondary Preaching Theme

The imagery from this section of Isaiah works well with the theme of Jesus's baptism, as it too describes the servant of the Lord as one in whom God has put God's Spirit. That spirit, Isaiah claims, leads the servant to bring forth justice on the earth—not through power and might, but through gentleness and a tireless pursuit of God's redemption and liberation for all the peoples of the earth. Isaiah isn't subtle about the pursuit of justice being central to the work of God in the world, and thus the preacher need not be either.

Call to Worship (Based on Isaiah 42:1-9)

The Lord's spirit is within us,
to bring justice to the nations.
Do not faint or grow weary,
until God's justice has been established on the earth.
I, the Lord, have called you for a good reason.
To be a light to the nations, to open blind eyes, to lead prisoners from prison, and those who sit in darkness from the dungeon.
Let us worship the God of justice.

Offertory Prayer/Prayer after Sermon

You are generous, O God, from the moment our life began and even to the grave. You have claimed as your own, and nothing can erase your love and embrace. Our gratitude overflows! Yet that love and embrace also comes with a calling: to proclaim and live your justice even to the ends of the earth. Grant us the courage to live adventurously for you, proclaiming and living your justice wherever we find ourselves and wherever liberation has yet to be made real. May the gifts we offer you this day be but the beginning of what we shall offer you with our lives and with our witness in the world. Amen.

Benediction

Friends, we have been "sealed by the Holy Spirit in baptism and marked as Christ's own forever." May the words we have spoken here this day be made visible in our lives. And may our lives bear witness to the truth that God loves all and desires justice and liberation for all creation. Go from this place to live at peace with your neighbors and to seek the welfare of all you pass this day and every day. Go in peace. Amen.

January 19, 2020–Second Sunday after Epiphany

Passages: Isaiah 49:1-7; Psalm 40:1-11; 1 Corinthians 1:1-9; John 1:29-42

Mark A. Miller

Gathering Prayer

Almighty God, make us be like John the Baptist, boldly proclaiming Jesus,
as the one who comes to take away the sins of the world.
Fashion us into instruments of your fierce and forgiving love.
Let the heavenly dove of the Spirit fall afresh on our weary souls, renewing us for the chal-
lenge of these days. We pray this in the name of the Eternal Holy One and Holy Three,
Creator, Christ, and Holy Spirit. Amen.

Preaching Theme

Have you ever been to a theater (or a high school auditorium) and seen those big old spotlights at the back of the room? Those long cylindrical contraptions are designed to have someone swivel and turn the light, to cast a flood of attention on a particular spot on the stage. Placed by the stage of the Jordan River, John the Baptizer was ready, prepared to shine the spotlight on the one who was coming to "take away the sins of the world." John saw his purpose, his life goal in proclaiming "make the Lord's path straight" and testifying of Jesus that "this one is God's Son."

In the passage immediately preceding John 1:29, John has the chance to take the glory for himself when he is interrogated by the Pharisees. Indeed, he says "I am not the Christ," but he *could* have said, "I might not be the Christ, but we are related—I am his cousin! I am the one who has been lifted up and blessed with the wisdom and insight to recognize the Holy when God reveals it!"

It might be tempting to think that we, as faithful clergy, worship leaders, or churchgoers, should be the ones people follow as their examples. After all, we have read the Bible, know the prayers and songs, and give our time, presence, gifts, and witness to the church. We must be closer to the Christ and therefore can be viewed as the role models for others. But to read this first passage of John is to be reminded that we are not in the spotlight. We are the ones pointing to the stage and crying, "Behold the Lamb of God!" We have the Baptizer to thank for this recognition of our calling and establishing the right relationship: We are all God's children, called not to be part of the "messiah club" but rather a priesthood of all believers, proclaiming God's faithfulness, mercy, justice, and love.

Secondary Preaching Themes

The Holy Spirit, present when John first proclaims Jesus as the Christ, is seen "coming down and resting" on Jesus "like a dove" in John 1. Later, the Holy Spirit, described in Acts 2, is like tongues of fire coming to "rest on each of them" gathered in the one place on the day of Pentecost. The Spirit's power, seen resting on Jesus at the Jordan River, is also found in community, where two or three are gathered in Jesus's name (cf. Matt 18:20). The characteristics of this divine gift might be described as the power to forgive and to bless.

Isaiah 49:1-7 shows us that God's calling is always beyond what we imagine. We are called to be servants of God; even before we were born, God called us to servanthood. And we are called to be reconcilers—to bring back disparate parts, as verse 5 says, "to restore Jacob to God, so that Israel might return to him." But we often set our sights too low in our calling to servanthood. God's calling is always bigger. It is too small a thing for us to be servants restoring *only* the tribes of Jacob and Israel. God will also make "you a light for the Gentiles, so that you could bring salvation to the end of the earth" (Acts 13:47).

Litany of Thanksgiving (Based on Psalm 40)

Together we waited patiently for the Lord and God heard our cry.
God drew us up from the desolate pit and set our feet upon a rock.
God put a new song in our mouths, a song of praise.
Happy are those who make the Lord their trust, who do not turn to the proud,
To those who go astray after false gods.
Be pleased, O Lord, to deliver us; O Lord, make haste to help us.
May all who seek you rejoice and be glad in you;
May those who love your salvation say continually, "Great is the Lord!"

Benediction

God, send us forth from this place proclaiming the good news of Jesus and his forgiving, saving love. Let our lives be a witness to the overflowing grace and mercy of your love. We pray it in the name of Jesus, the lamb of God. Amen.

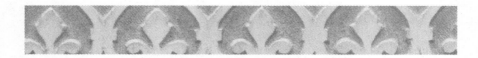

January 26, 2020–Third Sunday after Epiphany

Passages: Isaiah 9:1-4; Psalm 27:1, 4-9; I Corinthians 1:10-18; Matthew 4:12-23

Gary Simpson

Gathering Prayer

Loving and Leading God, today we pray for other churches open in your name. We confess that each church, including our own, is imperfect before you. But today we ask that each church flourish and encourage others in ways we cannot, and may none of the glory of any of our successes belong to anyone but you, for thine only is the kin-dom, the power and the glory. Amen.

Preaching Theme

Too often our church conversation is preoccupied with the particular concerns of our local fellowship. This text calls us to an appreciation of churches and believing communities beyond our particular locus. The Apostle Paul challenges us to see beyond the impulses of competitiveness. Too often our churches are replenished by the disgruntled or disaffected former members of other churches.

Both our church and every church belong to Jesus Christ. This passage gives every preaching pastor the opportunity to confess that she or he is not the source of the church's successes.

I once heard a pastor define the pastoral task in the congregation, saying that there are three groups of people in every church.

1. The people who genuinely love Jesus.
2. The people who genuinely love the pastor.
3. The people who have no love for Jesus or the pastor!

He went on to make this important observation: While we spend most of our time and energy on the people in the last category, our assignment is to work with the people who love us who have not yet met Jesus and get them to love Jesus. This is done by deflecting, confessing, and refocusing. This is Paul's pastoral strategy here.

Thank God for Chloe and her people. They are only mentioned here in the whole of the New Testament, yet they perform the great task of intercession and intervention for church communities in the crisis of competition. They seek the unity of the faith and yearn to stop the bickering among fellow believers.

Secondary Preaching Themes

Certainly in Isaiah 9:1-4, Psalm 27, and Matthew 4, the image of light and its relationship to darkness can be explored, but only if the preacher is to steer clear of weaponizing light over darkness in all things. This is dangerous in our present global context.[2]

Call to Worship

We find each other in the waters of our baptism.
No matter whose hand poured or dipped or sprinkled.
It is by the Spirit alone that the water makes us whole and makes us one.
It is only by God's power that we are named, claimed, and called Beloved.

Benediction

May we go, in the power of the water, to rise up, one body in Christ, to soothe and challenge an aching world.

February 2, 2020–Fourth Sunday after Epiphany

Passages: Malachi 3:1-4; Psalm 84 or Psalm 24:7-10; Hebrews 2:14-18; Luke 2:22-40

Karyn L. Wiseman

Focusing Prayer

Lord of Life, we gather on this day to remember the presence of the Spirit in our lives. We gather to hear the ways we are invited to live up to the call in our lives. We gather to celebrate the vision you place in our lives to move forward in faith. Grant us the insight of Simeon and Anna to walk into the wisdom and light of God. Amen.

Preaching Theme

One focus for this sermon is on the question of human potential. Jesus was seen by Simeon and Anna for what he would become. They saw God in him. They saw the good he would bring about. They saw the power of the Messiah in that little child. And his parents were amazed. When children are little, we almost all think our children are special. We brag about their accomplishments, we celebrate their victories, we offer them participation trophies for everything they do in order to boost their confidence, and we talk lovingly about their gifts. But if we were to really see into their future, we might change how we raise them. It's best to let them grow as they are intended. But it's also best to look beyond the surface and see the good that they can do. In this text we see parents amazed and possibly struggling with what has been told to them about their child. Imagine a baptism scene in the modern church when someone stands up and begins telling everyone about the adult life of the child. We, too, would be amazed by the talk they heard that day.

The reality is that everyone must eventually determine their own paths and how to use their gifts in the ways that have meaning for them. But I believe this: God has a lot invested in us; it's our job to live up to that potential. And the amazing part is that God loves us even when we fail. For your listeners, offer them the grace that is needed when we fail and the hope of living more into the potential we have. Let's help our listeners to be caught up in the arms of one who sees the potential in us all and empowers us to live more fully and profoundly into that life.

Secondary Preaching Theme

Another option is to look at the vivid presence of the Holy Spirit in this text. Simeon has been promised he will see the Messiah before his death. The Spirit leads Simeon to the temple and he then sees the arrival of Joseph and Mary to this holy place. Jesus's parents show their devotion and confidence in God by bringing Jesus for this special moment. And in that space and in that moment, we hear about the presence of the Spirit. Many in mainline denominations avoid talking about the Spirit, except maybe on Pentecost. But the Holy Spirit is a pivotal part of our faith experience.

When I was growing up, I thought the Holy Spirit was only talked about in Pentecostal or charismatic churches because I did not hear about it much in my United Methodist upbringing. As I have grown in years and in faith, the Holy Spirit has become a more pronounced part of my life and faith. As a preacher, I rely on the Spirit to encourage, inspire, and uphold me as I prepare *and* deliver my sermon. The people in your pews need to hear a word that will sustain them in their own faith journeys.

Do not be afraid to go to the well and the depths of the power that comes from the presence of the Holy Spirit. The connections of the primary preaching theme and this one are clear: The Spirit is part of living into the potential we all have. A life of discipleship requires trusting in our own God-given potential and living a life inspired by the power of the Holy Spirit.

Call to Worship

God has called us to gather and to celebrate the presence of the Spirit in our midst.
We come to hear the Word and to live more fully into our calling.
God of hope and life, empower us to love more fully and to serve more passionately.
We welcome the power of the Spirit to lead us into discipled lives.
God of grace and glory, encourage us to live up to the potential in our lives.
We gather to be fed so that we may live in grace and love with our neighbors everywhere. Amen and Amen

Benediction

Go with the power of the Spirit to live more fully into your potential as beloved children of God to serve the world. Amen.

February 9, 2020–Fifth Sunday after Epiphany

Passages: Isaiah 58:1-9a (9b-12); Psalm 112:1-9 (10);
1 Corinthians 2:1-12 (13-16); Matthew 5:13-20

Grant Hagiya

Gathering Prayer

God of love and righteousness, speak to us today your prophetic word that enables us to turn our lives around. Your divine love allows us to seek your righteousness that will be a taste of kin-dom to come. Do not give up on us, O Lord! Let us lead your people to a greater justice, even as we acknowledge our own complicity in the ways of our fallen world.

Preaching Theme

Isaiah 58:1-12 reminds us of the dual context in which we live. Remember: the Israelites are in exile, torn away from their home and suffering from their falling short of God's vision by being a conquered nation. But even in the stark reality of their oppression, they continue to harm each other by unjust practices and seeking selfish gain. So they cry "Lord, Lord" and yet turn their back on God by taking advantage of others for their own benefit. They falsely practice their faith through inauthentic fasts, practicing an "empty ritual" while "oppressing all their workers."

The fast that God chooses is one in which they will feed the hungry, provide a bed for the homeless, and clothe the poor. Only then will they be healed, as their light will shine in the darkness and flood their world with the glory of God. Those who know God act justly and righteously. God hears their cry of exile and will come to deliver them. How will they be allowed to go home if they only mirror the oppression that keeps them captive in the here and now?

So too we in the present time are living in a dual context. We live in a consumeristic society that values the things of the world, hungering for power, fame, fortune, and always more accumulations. Even the churches that we attend have been co-opted by desiring more—more people, money, reputation, and influence. In seeking these things, our fasts are hollow and empty. We long for real meaning in our lives, and more material possessions never satisfies us. As Christians, Jesus demands the same actions from us as the Israelites: feeding the hungry, providing shelter for the homeless, and clothing the naked. Only when we practice our faith in such a way will God hear our cries. Until then, we are in exile, foreigners in an alien land, looking to return home to God. Real spiritual meaning only comes when we reach out and care for the least of these in our midst: the poor, the prisoner, the immigrant, and any who are oppressed. In doing so, our light will shine forth, and God will send meaning and hope to flood our lives.

Secondary Preaching Themes

In the Epistle text from 1 Corinthians 2, we see the dual contexts between limited human wisdom and unlimited spiritual power from God. The unspiritual will never see the twin contexts we live in. This is only accessible by living in the mind of Christ, but we need to remember that no one in the secular world will understand us.

Likewise, in Matthew 5, when we care and tend to the least of God's creation our light shines forth for all to see. Our light is the good deeds we do, and some may give glory to God because people will see why we do such good.

Historian Rodney Stark reports that when the Black Plague ripped through the Roman Empire in 260 CE, Dionysius (Bishop of Alexandria) wrote that the non-Christians pushed those who suffered away and fled for their lives. Christians lived with the Easter conviction of another world instead. They had contempt for death. "Heedless of danger," writes Dionysius, "they took charge of the sick, attending to their every need and ministering to them in Christ, and with them departed this life serenely happy; for they were infected by others with the disease, drawing on themselves the sickness of their neighbors and cheerfully accepting their pains."[3]

Prayer of Confession

We confess, O Lord, living by the values of our secular world.
Forgive us and turn us to you.
We confess our turning to the wisdom of the world.
Forgive us and enable us to live by your spiritual power.
We confess we have not cared for the least and lost in our midst.
Forgive us and move us to compassion and care.
We confess that we more often conform to the ways of this world.
Forgive us and allow us into your spiritual presence.
We return to you with our hearts, minds, and spirits, praying together as Jesus taught:
(All recite the Lord's Prayer).

Benediction

Acknowledging the tension of our dual contexts, may we go now seeking to live by the Spirit—giving bread to the hungry and drink to the thirsty, clothing the naked, and visiting the sick and imprisoned. And may the love and grace of God sustain us all. Amen.

February 16, 2020–Sixth Sunday after Epiphany

Passages: Deuteronomy 30:15-20 or Sirach 15:15-20; Psalm 119:1-8; 1 Corinthians 3:1-9; Matthew 5:21-37

Grace Pak

Gathering Prayer (Inspired from Deut 30:15-20)

O God, you are the source of life, and all that is good comes from you. We gather today as our commitment to choose life and what is good. May you be glorified in our worship as we choose to love you, to walk in your ways and keep your words in our lives. May the Holy Spirit minister to us and enable us to continue to choose life by loving you, by obeying your voice, and by clinging to you with every breath. We pray in Jesus's name. Amen.

Preaching Theme

Today's Gospel lesson is a part of Jesus's Sermon on the Mount, which is not just a moral compass guiding the community life but also a guide to a worshipful life for believers. Worship is not limited to what happens in the sanctuary. Worship includes all aspects of our lives outside of sanctuary. The relationships we have, how we treat each other, and what we say and do express our faith in God. Thus being worshipful "out there" inspires true worship "in here."

And so Jesus instructs us to go and make things right with our brother or sister first and then come back and offer our gifts to God in worship. Furthermore, worshipful and faithful life "out there" requires decisiveness and commitment to take God's word seriously and hold ourselves accountable for our actions. What we say and do, even just looking at someone with improper thoughts and motivations, have consequences. They bring harm and disrupt worshipful life not just for us, but also to the other and the whole community. Thus, "if your right eye causes you to fall into sin, tear it out and throw it away...and if your right hand causes you to fall into sin, chop it off and throw it away" (vs. 29-30). Being worshipful "out there" inspires true worship "in here."

In what ways is Holy Spirit inviting you to commit your life to be worshipful "out there"? What does it mean to "make things right with your brother or sister"? What do you need to do to make things right? Who are your brother and sister?

Secondary Preaching Theme

Moses is nearing the end of his life. The Israelites are about to begin a new life in the Promised Land across the river. This is Moses's last opportunity to instruct his beloved people. "Now choose life—so that you and your descendants will live!" (Deut 30:19). Essentially, your life and the lives of your children depend on "loving the Lord your God by obeying his voice, and by clinging to him" (v. 20). Moses is clear: God is life. God is good. God is the source of life, and apart from God, there is death. However, to choose life, to choose God is not a one-time decision. It is not a one-time commitment. It begins at the point we make the decision to choose life, and that commitment is revisited and renewed every time we are faced with a decision, no matter how mundane and small it may be. To choose life, intentional decisions are made every day, every moment, to live and be according to God's commandments.

What would it mean for you to choose life daily? What does it look like to choose God day to day? In what ways have you experienced life as you chose God?

Prayer of Confession (Based on Psalm 119:1-8)

Holy God, you have given us your instruction and laws so that we can experience life that is truly happy. Forgive us for not seeking you with all our hearts. Forgive us for straying from your ways. Forgive us for not keeping your instructions most carefully. Strengthen us to keep your statutes and learn your righteous way. We will keep your words. Be near us, O merciful God! Amen.

Sending Forth

Our worship of God does not end now but continues on throughout the week at home, at work, at school, in marketplaces, at playgrounds, and wherever you are as you choose to live by God's words and commandments. May the Holy Spirit empower you and give you courage to choose life, choose to worship God every moment. In so doing, may God be glorified among you, through you, and in you. The blessings of God, the Father, Son and the Holy Spirit go with you! Amen.

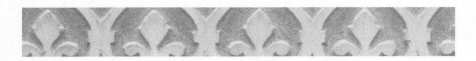

February 23, 2020–Seventh Sunday after Epiphany

Passages: Exodus 24:12-18; Psalm 99; 2 Peter 1:16-21; Matthew 17:1-9

Tanya Linn Bennett

Gathering Prayer

Can we look up? The mountains soar above us. Those mountains might be soaring stone crafted by earthquakes and shifting plates and wind and water. Those mountains might be the brick high-rises of our cities, the towers of office buildings, the places we live and work. But, no matter, on the horizon where the sun, the Son, rises, above these mountains, there we find our hope and our salvation.

Preaching Theme

Things happen on mountains. For over twenty summers, my good friend and colleague Mark Miller and I gathered around forty junior and senior high school students and some great musician-counselors for a summer music camp. Over the course of a week, we sang a lot, played a lot, talked a lot, and formed a community shaped by the values of inclusivity, honoring of every body and spirit, and Christian friendship. On the last night of camp, we traveled to the northern corner of the state of New Jersey, where New York, New Jersey, and Pennsylvania converge along the Appalachian Trail. In the stone pavilion constructed there as a resting place for those hiking the trail, we would join together in a picnic supper and watch as the sun sunk down into the mountains around it. One week, a crashing thunderstorm tracked its way across the mountains until it arrived at the pavilion, and brilliant lighting, booming thunder, and slashing rain surrounded us as we huddled in fear and awe at the power of God made manifest in this display of creation.

That was a singular weather event in all our years. But the consistent closing ritual that marked every single year was a love feast. We would form a big circle around the perimeter of the pavilion and pass whatever had been the standard fare of camp that week—usually water or bug juice and cookies. Before eating, each person in the circle would express their gratitude for what we had experienced together that week. We started by saying our names, which we would repeat back in affirmation. And then we would hear the stories of transfiguration—of notions of being changed from the inside out and prayers that this glow, this obvious work of the Spirit, would transfer back to where we had come from.

A calling out of the normal often allows for these "mountaintop experiences." But our rallying call at each of these love feasts was, "How does this sense of belonging, this bond of acceptance, this unconditional love and non-judgment become the norm in our lives every single day, no matter where we are?" Our prayer always was, "How do we become the bearers of goodness, mercy, and love that transfigures each and every space we enter?"

This is a critical message for our bodies of Christ gathering to hear a rallying cry in our houses of worship. Transfigured through mountaintop experiences, we go to shine in a world of dimness.

Secondary Preaching Theme

In a world of ambiguity and vague language, how do we translate rules written in stone for our daily lives (as in Exod 24)? Ethical decision-making with a lens that sees and considers the broader impact of what we say and do is much needed in our world. Can our churches be places that not only encourage this but teach and demonstrate it? In what ways are the Ten Commandments a guide or a hindrance to decision-making in this day and age?

Communion Setting

Great Prayer of Thanksgiving

Oh God, who leads us to the mountaintop time and time again, may this next time be the one when we are reshaped, inside out, glowing with your glory. We thank you that you never forget us or leave us alone, but come again and again with this spectacular possibility, a people remade, led from the shadows to stand in the streaming light of heaven.

Benediction

We go into the world to shimmer in the shadows,
the promise of God's love shining in our faces.
May we go in peace, in justice, and in joy.

February 26, 2020– Ash Wednesday

Passages: Isaiah 58:1-12; Psalm 51:1-17; 2 Corinthians 5:20b–6:10; Matthew 6:1-6, 16-21

Harriett Olson

Gathering Prayer (Based on Psalm 51)

Have mercy on me, God, according to your faithful love!
Wipe away my wrongdoings according to your great compassion!
Wash me completely clean of my guilt;
purify me from my sin!
Create a clean heart for me, God;
put a new, faithful spirit deep inside me!
Please don't throw me out of your presence;
please don't take your holy spirit away from me.
Return the joy of your salvation to me
and sustain me with a willing spirit.

Preaching Theme

I have always wondered about what the developers of the lectionary had in mind in assigning the Matthew passage and the other ones related to Ash Wednesday. For many Protestants, Ash Wednesday is one of the days that we do practice our religion publicly. Some of us receive the imposition of ashes. Many attend special services early in the morning, at noon, or in the evening, and some of us fast and begin a fasting pattern for the Lenten season. Surely the Scripture is not counseling against meaningful observances . . . or is it?

The Isaiah reading is helpful at this point. What exactly is the observance that God calls us to? After setting up the question, the prophet reports that justice, charity, and the honoring of obligations to others is the "fast" to which the righteous are called.

Surely the fasting should be connected to repentance. Rabbi Danya Ruttenberg has some challenging comments on what repentance, *tshuvah,* requires. Persons who have acted wrongly must first acknowledge the harm they have done and, second, undertake the work required to engage in internal, personal changes to become the kind of person who does not commit the same wrong. Then, restitution for the harm is appropriate (if possible, depending on the nature of the harm). Once this is done, then an apology to the victim is in order. The expectation is that this will result in a changed life and the offense will not be repeated.

I hear echoes of Jesus's instruction in Matthew 5:23-24 to leave your gift at the altar until you are reconciled with the person who has something against you. This puts repentance, restoration of relationship, and just living at the heart of practice of faithfulness. While fasting and ritual observances can be an aid to making time and space to examine ourselves, we are called to practice faithfulness at a much deeper level.

Secondary Preaching Themes

A somewhat different tone in the call for righteousness is heard in the Isaiah passage. Here the prophet levels a critique against the community, rather than talking purely about personal transgressions. This is a call to reform our collective way of life, and may provide some balance to a very individualistic awareness of personal guilt. We should grieve and repent for the failure to commit ourselves as a community to abundant life for all. The passage from 2 Corinthians also sounds a bit different when we remind ourselves that this is a letter to the community begging them to be reconciled to God for the sake of God's purpose: reconciling the whole world to himself through Christ (2 Cor 5:19). Inviting the community to this sort of work is a practice or pattern of life—not just a day or a season.

Worship Helps

If the service will focus on introspection and beginning a process of repentance for individual sin, the worship space could be somewhat darker than usual with appropriate worship music. Consider providing space for actual reflection and not filling the service with words. If the service will include reflection on local, regional, national, or global injustice, then focus information could be provided in a bulletin or in stations around the worship space. More light will be needed in the setting, and the call might be to create a common list of potential actions that could be taken collectively in the process of repentance.

Prayer of Repentance

Consider a bidding prayer, with time for persons to reflect and pray. If the congregation has a tradition of writing things on a piece of paper to be burned or otherwise disposed of, that can be incorporated here.

I invite you into a time of prayer in the posture of repentance. Please use the pauses between each phrase as a time to make your own confession, prompted by the spoken phrase.

Merciful God, we confess that we have not loved you with our whole heart.
[pause for 30 seconds or more]
We have failed to be an obedient church. [pause]
We have not done your will. [pause]
We have broken your law. [pause]
We have rebelled against your love. [pause]
We have not loved our neighbors and we have not heard the cry of the needy. [pause]
Forgive us, we pray, and free us for joyful obedience, through Jesus Christ our Lord. Amen.

Benediction

This night [or day] and this season we enter a journey of repentance. We undertake this journey as a response to God's offer of reconciliation through the life, death, and resurrection of Jesus Christ. Though the journey will take time, we embark with full confidence because Jesus, who is our judge and our measure, has already proved his love for us. Go forth in faith, with the confidence that it is this loving God who calls us and goes before us. Amen.

March 1, 2020–First Sunday in Lent

Passages: Genesis 2:15-17; Psalm 32; Romans 5:12-19; Matthew 4:1-11

LaTrelle Easterling

Opening Prayer

Holy and blessed God, we praise your holy name and give thanks for your abundant grace and mercy. As we enter this season of Lent, we desire to center ourselves in the fullness of this moment. We are embarking upon a familiar journey, and yet it is unchartered territory. Free us from the chains of liturgical routine. Awaken us to a deeper experience. Draw us beyond superficial repentance; draw us beyond our preconceived understandings; draw us beyond our certitude; draw us home to our truest selves, to the beloved community and to you.

Preaching Theme

The book of Genesis offers deep metaphors for the season of Lent, a season of reflection, repentance, and renewal. These passages teach a timeless lesson on God's provision and desire for deep communion with humanity. These verses also shine a light on the destructive consequences of egotism and selfishness.

When God breathed God's *pneuma* into dust and placed those souls in the garden, a full and perfect relationship of love, communion, and trust was created. Through the gifts of collaboration and community, they were empowered to be in relationship with creation, to tend and enhance creation. The equilibrium and sacredness of the garden was interrupted when humanity succumbed to the temptation of self-aggrandizement over against complete trust in and reliance on God. A forest of shame borne of the seed of selfishness then separated humanity from full communion with their creator. What selfish motivations are wreaking havoc in our personal lives, churches, and communities? Where have we given sway to egotism over an abiding communion with God? How might our lives be more peaceful and fruitful if we resisted destructive temptations?

In our postmodern Christian discernment, there is often a tension between whether sin or love is the overarching message of our faith. Genesis offers a both/and response. God is love, and yet the depth and breadth of God's love cannot be fully understood without acknowledging the presence of sin. Perhaps our disdain for acknowledging sin rests in the failure to tell the rest of the story. After acknowledging their actions, God does not respond with consequences alone; rather, God also continues to offer provision. How can we fully explore the message of Genesis without the overworked either/or analysis?

Lent offers a precious opportunity to reexamine God's intent for creation, to earnestly repent of our sin and renew our covenant. As we journey these forty days and nights, the beloved community has the opportunity to become the church God envisioned. As we do, the church then becomes the place where others who are broken can find wholeness. Those seeking deliverance, healing, hope, and love can experience the transformative inertia of the church's blessing.

Secondary Preaching Theme

The themes of temptation, trust, and humility are highlighted in Matthew 4:1-11. In juxtaposition to the actions and attitude in the garden, the writer of Matthew illustrates the faithfulness of Christ as he humbly relied upon God and God's word. Even in his starvation, Christ demonstrates the strength inherent in feasting upon every word of God rather than the empty words of humanity. Another prescient theme to be explored is the problem of half-truths. How did knowing the fullness of God's word enable Jesus to withstand temptation? What strength can be drawn from the humility of relying on God's word as we wrestle with the demons in our lives?

Guided Meditation (Inspired by Psalm 32)

We sit in the liminality between Ash Wednesday and Easter, the already and the not yet of our faith. We know the depth of your love for us, and the ways we have both received and resisted that love. May we sit in your holiness and breathe. . . .

We acknowledge your love for us, as we desire to experience you even more fully.

We are too often imprisoned by our pasts, mistakes, disappointments, and sin. The weight of it is too heavy. Rejoice people of God! Our creator offers a fresh start; our slates are wiped clean. May we breathe in your forgiveness. . . .

When we kept it all inside, our bones wore out, our groans echoed endlessly. We admit our sin and rejoice in the newness of life.

The faithful should pray during times of trouble and not run from our God. May we breathe in your sheltering embrace. . . .

In our darkest hour you are our refuge from the storm. You offer chords of comfort swelling to a symphony of safety.

May we continually confess before the God of our creation, to empty ourselves of the burden of brokenness and pain. May we come again and again as empty vessels before a full fountain to be filled with hope, reconciliation, and peace.

Benediction

Breathe deeply of God's forgiveness. Breathe deeper still of God's grace. Let the fullness of it flow through our bodies and become reality in our consciousness. Let the shalom of God be our guide as we renew our covenant of discipleship.
May it be so. Amen.

March 8, 2020–
Second Sunday in Lent

Passages: Genesis 12:1-4a; Psalm 121; Romans 4:1-5, 13-17; John 3:1-17

Heather Murray Elkins

Gathering Prayer

Sisters and brothers,
the living God,
the God who never forgets,
calls us to remember.
Our help comes from the Holy One,
maker of heaven and earth.
Sisters and brothers,
the living God,
the God who always remembers,
calls us to rejoice.
We are standing on holy ground
and we do not stand alone.
Our God is a mighty God who was and is and will be forever!

Preaching Theme

John's Gospel begins with primal symbols of darkness and light, and these are interwoven into descriptions of the physical settings of Jesus's ministry as well as spiritual conditions. There is a difference between night and day, and John's Jesus insists that the reader, the hearer, the believer must choose. There are no shades of grey in this test of discipleship or in this familiar text. "This is the judgment: the light has come into the world, but people preferred darkness to light because their deeds were evil" (3:19 NRSV).

Nicodemus, a respected leader and teacher, comes under the cover of darkness to ask the hard question: "Is it possible that everything I know is wrong?" He clearly recognizes the signs of God in Jesus; he knows wisdom when he hears it, but that wisdom is making a fool of him. He's an old teacher who is still hungry to learn, but he doesn't expect to be demoted to preschool. Jesus doesn't make it easy. He uses the one word for "birth," *anothen,* that has two different meanings: "born again" or "reborn" and "born from above." Nicodemus goes for the literal, turning the Spirit's work into a laborious affair.

John's Jesus is a code talker, using symbolic language to distinguish between those who are children of light and those who have chosen the shadowland. If we draw back from this dramatic staging between this teacher of the law and the One who is Wisdom, we can also hear the post-Easter community of John speaking to the religious authorities who were colluding with Rome to ostracize converts to Christianity. "I assure you that we speak about what we know and testify about what we have seen, but you don't receive our testimony" (3:11).

Leaders like Nicodemus may be the spiritual guardians of the holy of holies, but they resemble the Romans trying to guard an empty tomb. "God's Spirit blows wherever it wishes. You hear its sound, but you don't know where it comes from or where it is going. It's the same with everyone who is born of the Spirit" (3:8).

It seems that Nicodemus doesn't appreciates the lesson or the question. He simply slips away into the night, disappears from the Gospel scene. But in the darkest moment for the followers of Jesus, Nicodemus shows up again. It is Nicodemus and Joseph of Arimathea who anoint and wash Jesus's body and prepare it with spices for burial. It's an intimate and courageous witness. Near the Gospel's end, Nicodemus steps out of the shadows into the public square of Rome's empire and choses the Light (19:39-42).

Secondary Preaching Themes

The images of pilgrimage and the language of the Spirit's new birth are linked in these scriptural texts in the season of Lent. Both present the reader/hearer/believer a choice. Do you trust the One who is the Way? Will you begin a pilgrimage of faith, filled with assurance of the God who guards and shelters? Have you been born by water and the Spirit? Both scripture passages offer the believer life filled with assurance and the power of the Spirit.

This theme of assurance connects this Lenten gospel and this psalm. Fanny Crosby's hymn "Blessed Assurance" would provide the musical affirmation of faith in a trustworthy God and Jesus, the Christ. This is story filled with assurance of the God who guards like a mother and shelters like a father. This is the song of a child of God, an "heir of salvation" in and through Christ. We are "born of his spirit" and this is our story and our song.

Prayer (Following Reading of Psalm 121)

Holy One, El Shaddai
In the valleys of Lent
we lift up our eyes to the hills and ask,

"Where is our hope?"
Our hearts echo your answer:
"I am your help in all times and spaces."

If we stumble on the Way
You will not let us fall.
Your love is our shelter
no matter the storm.

When our days seem stark and empty
and nights too dark or long,
You watch with us as the light rises
and gift us with a heart for singing
from this time and forever more.

Suggested Hymn

"Blessed Assurance" by Fanny J. Crosby, *The United Methodist Hymnal*, 369

Call/Response (Before Reading of Gospel)

Dearly Beloved,
What do you see?
The shadows are deep
But the Light is rising.
Dearly Beloved,
What do you believe?
Christ has redeemed us.
The Spirit has set us free!

March 15, 2020–
Third Sunday in Lent

Passages: Exodus 17:1-7; Psalm 95; Romans 5:1-11; John 4:5-42

Lydia Muñoz

Gathering Prayer

O Come! Let the wild rumpus begin! Let the joyful noise and grateful praise ring out! For God is great, the Creator of the Universe is marvelous and is here! Once we were no people, but now we are One people gathered together to sing out God's praise and live out God's justice. O Come! Let the praises ring out and let the wild rumpus begin!

Preaching Theme

There are usual suspects that come first to our minds when reading this pericope in John. Over the years, I've heard them all: the woman with five husbands, Jesus and the Samaritan, the adulterer turned evangelist…and so on. None of these are bad but, frankly, they're unoriginal, and, as a woman, I dread the references. But what if instead of looking at this passage as an indictment of this woman's sexual lifestyle, we focus on the things not said.

A great theologian, sister, and mentor, Dr. Loida Martell-Otero, said to me once, "You have to learn to read scripture against the grain and discover the things that are not on the surface but below it." In her former life, she was a large animal veterinarian in Puerto Rico, and she always reminded us that when examining animals, veterinarians always run their hands against the grain of the animal's skin and coat, slowly and methodically to see if they discover bumps and bruises that can't be seen on the surface. What if we did the same here?!

If the woman's reputation is so bad, that she has to come out to get water at a certain time of day, then how is it that instead of turning away from the conversation with Jesus, a man who is not a Samaritan, she instead engages with him in deep theological conversation as though she had every right to be there, defending her well and defending her way of worship? She never backs down from Jesus's conversation and instead allows him to enter into her space so that he can discover things about her own life.

Second, I've often wondered that if she indeed had such a bad standing with the community, how is it that upon her encounter with Jesus, she runs and tells the entire village and they follow her to come and see this man who has told her everything about herself? Sometimes we read a lot of our own biases into the text; there really is nothing in there that can confirm that she was an immoral woman, and it's really not hard to do, given how we have been shaped to believe about women in general, especially in scripture. The harder task is to go against the grain and see her not through our eyes, but perhaps through Jesus's. Do you know how incredible it feels when someone sees who you really are and recognizes the value that you bring to this world? It's as refreshing as a drink of living water.

Secondary Preaching Theme

Just like Jesus, Moses finds himself in need of provision for the people who are in the middle of the wilderness called Sin (how's that for a theme?). Water as an overall theme is an important spiritual symbol. Water is creative, and water is restorative. Water is destructive and can demolish, as we have seen in Puerto Rico, Florida, and other places around the world. Water can also be a symbol of justice and righteousness, and the renewing peace of God that restores the strength of all people who are thirsty and seeking a way out of their own wilderness experience. If we are talking about the life-giving water that God can provide, we can be sure that with it comes change. Clearly the people who are arguing and fussing with Moses aren't ready for the change, even though they had found themselves in the midst of slavery and oppression, but Moses hasn't given up on them and neither has God. Is that why they call it life-giving water, because grace never runs dry? During this season of Lent, the challenge will be whether or not we allow this life-giving stream to transform and create in us a new heart and a new life.

Call to Worship (Based on Psalm 95)

We, who are thirsty, gather at the Rock for Salvation.
Life-giving Spirit, quench our thirst!
Come, let us worship and kneel before the Lord, our Maker.
Life-giving Spirit, quench our need for peace!
Let's come before our God with thanks and songs of joy.
Life-giving Spirit, quench our need for justice!

Benediction (Based on John and Romans 5:1-11)

Beloved, we have been made right with God not on our own merit.
We have tasted the water of life and it is good.
Beloved, we have found peace with God through Christ.

We have drunk from the cup of salvation and it is good.
Beloved, we may face troubles that test our character, but we have this hope:
The everlasting, life-giving Spirit of Christ is always with us.
And it is good!

Suggested Hymn

Consider closing the worship experience with Israel Houghton's "Lord, You are Good," from the album *New Season*, 2001. CCLI, 3383788

March 22, 2020– Fourth Sunday in Lent

Passages: 1 Samuel 16:1-13; Psalm 23; Ephesians 5:8-14; John 9:1-41

Kathleen Stone

Gathering Prayer

Holy One, you created us. Our hearts are held by you. Every day from the beginning of our lives, we are doused with your mercy and love. There is nothing more we need. Help us today to see your way with us so that we become the beauty you intended. For the sake of ourselves and the world around us, in the middle of this very complex and difficult world and work, we sit beside the still water's presence. Flow through us, for the sake of your life-giving word. Amen.

Preaching Theme

Lent has often been seen as a time of intense self-reflection. But self-reflection without understanding the power that God holds to make something beautiful of our clay vessels, our little lives, is to defy the power of the God of Love. According to the psalmist, the valley of the shadow of death *is* where God is. It is in the presence of our enemies that a table is set, and, deep in our own muck, we are led beside the still waters. According to the book of Samuel, God picks David, a young child, to fight Goliath and to be king of all Israel. And through that kingship, which has its times of horror and times of victory, God makes David the king Israel needed for the moment. In addition, in the Gospel of John, the blind man suffers consistently throughout his life because people look at him as deficient, as sinful, as someone not worthy. Self-reflection in all these cases would bring us to a place of despair, but in the hands of a good and merciful God? Something beautiful happens.

As human beings, we look at vulnerabilities as weaknesses, as those places that need to be thrown out or erased, denied, or refused.... But it's in our weakness and vulnerabilities that God reveals God's self. It was in the choice of the smallest and youngest son that God revealed the king. It was in the valley of the shadow of death and in the presence of enemies that the poet knew that his God anointed him with the most fragrant oil and his cup ran over. And it was in the man's blindness that the Holy One's spit and a little mud helped him see.

But we live in a world where the expectation is that we are always and forever at the top of our game or we are punished. We live in a world where admitting our weakness is to admit defeat and to encourage harassment. We are in a world where we hide our hurt or we will be further damaged. And God says, "It's in our vulnerabilities that we find the grace" and that finding grace and mercy is the ultimate goal of human existence within the Christian faith. John Wesley hoped we would become perfected, but being perfected meant perfected in receiving and showing mercy, not in our perfection in a particular moral code or a sense of our own "doing it right." That is the transformative power of the Christian faith. The ability to receive and swim through the muddy and spit-filled complexity of life with a merciful, loving creator.

Secondary Preaching Theme

The blind man could have been a "seeing" man—it is not the healing of the man's blindness that is the ultimate experience Jesus hoped to address. The ultimate experience is God making us whole; God's work is in making us whole. The one who was blind from birth was surprised by grace, surprised by Jesus, shockingly loved and chosen, and his vulnerability became the place where the good news that he, too, was deeply loved was made manifest. The real injury in the blind man's life was the criticism from society, the damning from the religious leaders, and the selling out of his parents.

The ultimate holy experience, and one that is throughout scripture, is to experience God as one who does not see as mortals see—who does not see us in all the ways others have judged us, raced us, held us down, and been aggressively jealous or arrogant toward us. Yet it is facing those judgments, oppressions, imprisonments, jealousies, and arrogances, and reflecting and focusing on God's love, grace, and mercy that will heal us. The ultimate is that we are all yet beautiful, full, alive, living this life with the Spirit of God deep in our hearts. The ultimate is that God chose to birth us from love and mercy, continues to love and give us mercy every day of our lives, and, at the end of our life, will receive us into arms of love and mercy.

Experiential Worship Element

Hand out paper or strips of sheet blindfolds to everyone and have them write on the blindfold the quality or experience that keeps them personally away from a joyful receipt of mercy. (It's important to use a pen or marker that does not bleed through the strips). Have them put it over their eyes with the word hidden, on the inside of the strip. Pause for a minute or so in silence. Have participants remove the blindfold. Then, on the other side, have them write "MERCY" and put it back on with MERCY facing outward. And have them turn toward their neighbor in the pew.

Each of us have vulnerabilities and hurts. God is always Mercy. What we need from ourselves and one another is mercy. This is what we need to bring with us into the world.

March 29, 2020– Fifth Sunday in Lent

Passages: Ezekiel 37:1-14; Psalm 130; Romans 8:6-11; John 11:1-45

Editor's Note:
Two different approaches to the texts for the Fifth Sunday in Lent are offered here. Both grapple with themes of life and death as we approach Holy Week, the crucifixion, and the resurrection.

Drew Dyson

Gathering Prayer (Based on Psalm 130)

I hope, Lord.
My whole being hopes,
and I wait for God's promise.
My whole being waits for my Lord—
more than the night watch waits for morning;
yes, more than the night watch waits for morning!

Preaching Theme

Exhausted. Devastated. Frustrated. Knowing the human condition as we do, and being familiar with our own patterns of grief, it is easy to imagine the emotions Mary and Martha were experiencing at the death of their brother, Lazarus. During his illness, they sent word to Jesus that his friend was ill, and they waited expectantly for his return and for the healing that they knew would take place. After all, they had witnessed and heard of the healings of the royal official's son, the paralyzed man by the pool of Bethsaida, and the man born blind. It was their turn. Surely he would come.

Now, after several days have passed and their brother has died, Jesus strolls into town. Martha is the first to greet him, "Lord, if you had been here, my brother wouldn't have died." One gets the sense that the greeting is real. It is raw. It is unvarnished. Mary's encounter with Jesus echoed that of her sister. This time there was no oil to anoint his head...there were no tears to wipe with her hair...there was simply the utterance, "Lord, if you had been here..."

The story unfolds, as we know, with the dramatic scene of Jesus calling Lazarus forth from the tomb after he lay dead for four days. The miraculous healing clearly points to the power of God to overcome even the sting of death. The delayed unfolding of this miracle points to the difference between God's timing and human timing. While both excellent themes on which to preach, I believe that there is a powerful sermon at work in the courageous witness of these two sisters who unabashedly and authentically reveal their deep anger and disappointment in the face of the seeming absence of "the healer" from the first half of their story.

With the psalmist, the women sing, "I cry out to you from the depths, LORD— my LORD, listen to my voice!" (Ps 130:1-2). There is something profound in that their authentic expression reflecting their deepest anger and fear was a precursor to the healing of their brother. By opening themselves up fully to Jesus, they were able to receive the gift that awaited them. For Mary and Martha, that healing gift was the resurrection of their brother. For others, like myself following the recent death of my brother at an early age, the healing unfolds more gradually through restored familial relationships and inner peace.

In either case, the healing we long for often begins with our willingness to be real with our God—real about our anger, real about our disappointment, real about our fear. "Lord, if only you had been here...."

Secondary Preaching Theme

The eighth chapter of Paul's letter to the Romans is a commanding reflection on the work of the Holy Spirit in the lives of Christ followers. Romans 8:11 opens a powerful sermonic moment as we are reminded that the very same Spirit that raised Jesus from the dead lives in us. The same Spirit that hovered over the waters in creation (Gen 1:1-2)d...the same Spirit that redeemed Israel, appointing and anointing prophets, priests, and kings...the same Spirit by which Jesus performed miracles and proclaimed the kingdom of God...the same Spirit that raised Jesus from the dead – That same Spirit lives in you!

This sermon is an opportunity to highlight the work of the Holy Spirit in your church and in your community, leading to powerful questions to leave with your hearers: "If you believe that the same Spirit lives in you, how will you respond? What will you do?"

Call to Worship

Cry out to the Lord from the depths of your being;
Lord, listen to my voice! Pay attention to the yearning of my soul.
Hope in the Lord;
My whole being hopes, and I wait for the promise of God.

Benediction

We cry out, "Lord, if only you were here..." and we are reminded, "Lo, I am with you always." And so we go forth from this place with praise on our lips, for God has heard our cries and walks with us along the way. And as we go, may the love of the Holy One who hears our longing hearts, the grace of Jesus Christ who heals our brokenness, and the power of the Spirit who dwells in us, be with us this day and every day. Go in peace and may the peace of God go with you.

March 29, 2020– Fifth Sunday in Lent

Passages: Ezekiel 37:1-14; Psalm 130; Romans 8:6-11; John 11:1-45

Laurie Zelman

Gathering Prayer

Breath of Life, as we walk through this season of Lent, help us to rise up from within the dark valleys in our lives. Fill us with vision, turn us toward hope, for our life is in you. Amen.

Preaching Theme

Ezekiel is sent by God into the valley of dry bones, a place filled with death and hopelessness. We sense him looking down in shock as he realizes that he is walking over the remnant of a people. I am reminded of a description of the Kensington area of Philadelphia by *The Philadelphia Inquirer* reporters: "Tens of thousands of used syringes and their tossed-off orange caps cover the sloping ground like a plague of locusts . . . even some police officers are reluctant to traverse the embankment to get to the . . . overdose victims at the bottom."[1] We are surely in a dark valley as we begin to feel the effects of the plague that is the present and future opioid crisis.

God called Ezekiel to a vision of a people resurrected from dry and gruesome death and restored by degrees to a company of the living. Just as surely, God is calling the church to reach out with the vision of restoration for the millions of families stricken with addiction and the tragedy of overdose death. God tells Ezekiel that the house of Israel is saying, "Our bones are dried up, and our hope has perished. We are completely finished" (Ezek 37:11). Scientific research in the counseling profession has validated over and over again that one of the most critical functions a counselor provides is the engendering of hope. The church is charged with the same vision that God gave to Ezekiel: the Spirit breathes new, rich, joyous life: "I've spoken, and I will do it. This is what the Lord says" (37:14).

Secondary Preaching Theme

The story of Lazarus presents a powerful personal parallel to the resurrection of a hopeless people from valley of dry bones. In current legal terminology, an individual is dead if he or she has sustained irreversible cessation of circulatory and respiratory or brain functions. As I read the story of Lazarus in the tomb, it is in my mind to quibble with whether Lazarus was "really dead." But in some ways that is beside the point.

Scientists at the Albert Einstein College of Medicine are researching built-in timers in cells that predetermine when the cells will no longer be able to replicate—in other words, when they will die, leading to aging and death.[2] This means we all carry death within us, and indeed, life is full of losses and "little deaths," such as loss of relationships, jobs, homes, health, and loved ones. But just as we carry death within us, we can open to the voice of Jesus calling us into life.

Call to Worship

God calls us here:
God calls us to life.
God gives us dreams and hopes:
God calls us to life.
Breathe your breath into us, O Lord!
Let us live in you.
Let us worship the Giver of Life!

Suggested Hymn

"Hold Fast"[3]

When sons and daughters caught in chains
Let your people go
Cry out to end the searing pain
Let your people go

Refrain
Hold on, children
Hold fast for God will come
Breathing life and mercy
To let the people go

We tried to find an easy place
Let your people go
And found a counterfeit for grace
Let your people go

Hold on, children
Hold fast for God will come
Breathing life and mercy
To let the people go

Hear our broken, helpless cries
Let the people go
Spirit give us breath to rise
Let your people go

Hold on, children
Hold fast for God will come
Breathing life and mercy
To let the people go.

April 5, 2020–Palm and Passion Sunday

Passages: Isaiah 50:4-9a; Psalm 31:9-16; Philippians 2:5-11; Matthew 26:14–27

Sudarshana Devadhar

Gathering Prayer

O Holy One, as we observe Palm Sunday and enter into the Holy Week, we give you thanks for your mighty grace by which you offered us salvation through the ministry and mission of Jesus Christ.

May this week help us to experience the depth of your love in our own lives. May we experience this week, not as our custom or tradition, but as our dying with Christ that like him, we will rise to a new spring, truly empowered by the Holy Spirit. We ask this in the precious name of our Lord and Savior Jesus Christ. Amen.

Preaching Theme

This famous christological hymn (Phil 2) offers various possibilities for reflecting on our Christian baptismal calling as disciples of Jesus Christ. It challenges us to mirror Christ's ministry in our own lives or, in the words of St. Paul, to "adopt the attitude that was in Christ Jesus" (v. 5).

What was that attitude?

First, "Though he was in the form of God, he did not consider being equal with God something to exploit" (v. 6). The church often has a tendency to elevate the man of Christ to the rank of God, which Christ did not do himself. Instead, Christ reminds us throughout the Gospels that he came not as a substitute for God but instead to fulfill the mission of God.

Second, in fulfilling this mission, Christ "emptied himself by taking the form of a slave and by becoming like human beings" (v. 7). It is only when we empty ourselves by letting go of our egos, arrogance, and pride, and display a willingness to perform menial tasks for the well-being of others, truly filled with the spirit of humility, that we make a difference in the world as witnesses of Christ.

Third, he became "obedient to the point of death, even death on a cross" (v. 8). This reminds us that the size of our salaries, the diplomas we hang on our walls, and our popularity will not define our ministry and mission, but our willingness to exchange our crown for the cross will.

Finally, at the end, it was Christ's faithfulness to his calling that led him to be "highly honored" by God (v. 9). St. Teresa, a woman who lived her Christian baptism with a Christlike attitude, articulated it well when she said that Christian ministry is not about success, but about faithfulness.

Secondary Preaching Themes

How can we develop the attitude of Christ? Perhaps one place from which to draw some insight is the prophet Isaiah in chapter 50, who acknowledges that it is "the LORD God [who] gave me an educated tongue to know how to respond to the weary" (v. 4). Because Isaiah was trusting God completely, he could say boldly, "Look! The LORD God will help me. Who will condemn me? Look, they will wear out like clothing; the moth will eat them" (v. 9). The question for all of us is whether we trust in God as Isaiah did. Are we willing to listen to the voice and guidance of God? As a part of this calling, we also need to be brutally honest with one another. Jesus became vulnerable by telling his disciples what he was going through and asking them to be in prayer with God. Though there are many sub-themes in the Passion Narrative, we need to acknowledge that in order to be faithful for the *kairos* moment in his ministry, Jesus once again had to go into deep, deep prayer and trust in the power of God through his entire trial and crucifixion. The question we need to ask again and again is what the significance of prayer is in our own lives.

Benediction

May the God who called Isaiah, Jesus, St. Teresa, and scores of others challenge, stimulate, and empower you to enter into the Holy Week, so you may demonstrate the love of Christ and be filled with the Holy Spirit. May you experience anew the attitude of Christ, so others may glorify God because of your Christian witness. May people experience Christ in new ways through your life. Amen.

April 9, 2020– Maundy Thursday

Passages: Exodus 12:1-4, (5-10), 11-14; Psalm 116:1-2, 12-19;
1 Corinthians 11:23-26; John 13:1-17, 31b-35

James McIntire

Gathering Prayer

Not only my feet, O God, but also my hands and my head. May I be washed in your Word and faithful in my words. Amen.

Preaching Theme

Maundy Thursday. The anticipation and disappointment, the table and the meal, the sounds and the silence, the light and dark, the gathering and dispersing. The evening and the texts lend themselves to dramatic retelling of this essential story.

This night doesn't require sermonizing, as the texts and drama and symbols tell the story quite nicely, so it may very well be an opportunity to lean into the apocryphal saying of St. Francis: "Preach the Gospel at all times. When necessary, use words." But if you feel like you must preach, the theme of the Gospel text that lends its name to the description—*mandatum novum*, new commandment—can be the theme for the night. "I give you a new commandment: Love each other. Just as I have loved you, so you also must love each other. This is how everyone will know that you are my disciples, when you love each other" (John 13:34-35).

The "love each other" commandment is the standard by which can be measured all that we say and do as followers and disciples of Jesus. Is excluding someone from the church loving them? No. Is waging war against others loving them? No. Is allowing some to go hungry while others are sated loving them? No. Is creating rules and regulations that restrict who's in and who's out loving them? No. The text of this night and the theme for the worship experience is the core of the Jesus message—"love each other"—and is that on which everything else rests (see also Matt 22:36-40).

Experiment with that message in all you do in preparing and presenting this night. Ask of yourself and your congregation the Pesach Haggadah question of the youngest at the Seder table: "Why is this night different from all other nights?" For the followers of Jesus then and now, this night is the pivot in the Passion Narrative to the centrality of that new commandment.

Consider how different voices might highlight the emotions of the evening—a scripted shared reading of dialogue, a narrator moving the scene along, a descriptive voice setting the environment. These don't need to be professional actors or vocal artists but ordinary people like the disciples. Encourage people to feel what's going on at the table and what thoughts and emotions they might experience in a similar setting. Gather ahead of time for a read-through so people can hear themselves and each other.

Consider the setting for worship. For most, this is an evening worship experience. People might be seated around tables covered in purple or white cloths set in the form of a cross, candles down the table centers, palm branches from the Sunday before strewn around the tables or the floor. Play with the senses. The scent of candles, perfumed oil, or food can heighten the experience. (Be aware of any fragrance sensitivities in the group.) Quiet music or dramatic sounds can add to the evening—simple piano, recorded music, a capella hymns, or Taizé arrangements.

Consider including a foot washing element as the primary focus or one piece of the liturgy. Some are hesitant about exposing their feet or being touched in this way, so you might offer the option of water being poured over hands and then dried. You might have one person assist in holding the basin while you pour water and use the towel to dry. Or you might invite people to wash the feet of the one sitting beside them. If circumstances don't allow for the ritual, it can still be noted symbolically with a pitcher, basin, and towel as the centerpiece of the table.

Consider having this be a Tenebrae (from the Latin for "shadows") experience as candles are extinguished while the Passion Narrative is read aloud, leading to full darkness until the Christ candle reappears. It can be used to dim the mood after Palm Sunday's joyous celebration and prepare the congregation for Good Friday at the cross, Saturday in the tomb, and the resurrection celebration of Sunday.

Consider what the meal looks like. This might be an opportunity for a simple meal around tables—soup, bread, water—followed by sharing the bread and cup later in the evening. Or perhaps this is an opportunity to explain the Passover Seder, while also acknowledging that the texts are ambiguous about whether this evening was the Passover meal and the fact that the Seder as it is known today might not have been in common practice at the time the event happened or the texts written. (Be sensitive to not co-opt the Jewishness of the Seder and try to wrap around it a Christian interpretation of the ritual. Explain the purpose and context for a Seder within Judaism and let its symbols speak for themselves.) Or maybe the meal for tonight is simply the bread and cup in the midst of the liturgy.

Secondary Preaching Theme

The Corinthians text is arguably the oldest retelling of the Last Supper in liturgical form as it was used in the church at Corinth. If we began the season with the "Invitation to the Observance of Lenten Discipline" on Ash Wednesday and its call "to observe a holy Lent: By self-examination and repentance…" then Paul's reminder to "examine yourselves, and only then eat of the bread and drink of the cup" (11:28 NRSV) is a fitting reminder at the conclusion of the season.

Opening Prayer

Be with us this night, O God.
Be our strength as we face
our fears, our anxieties, our inadequacies.
Be our guide through the shadows
and a light to lead us from darkness.
Be present at table with us, we pray,
despite our failings, our denials, our betrayals.
In Christ. Amen.

Prayer after the Meal

From your table, O God,
send us filled by your presence,
send us to a world in need,
send us to a new life.
As you give yourself to us in this meal,
so let us now give ourselves for others.
In love you gave;
in love we receive;
in love we go. Amen.

April 10, 2020–Good Friday

Passages: Isaiah 52:13–53:12; Psalm 22; Hebrews 10:16-25; John 18:1–19:42

Vicki Flippin

Gathering Prayer

Crucified One, in the garden, around the charcoal fire, on the road to Golgotha, and all around us, temptations promise distraction from the pain, the grief, the injustice in our midst. Give us the strength to stay with you today, to walk through the valley of the shadow of death . . . with you. Amen.

Preaching Theme

Recently I was dropping off my child at preschool, and one of the other children was having a particularly difficult time saying good-bye to his father. Even before we walked into the building, we could hear the cries and screams of the troubled tot. "Daddy! Daddy!" Inside the classroom, I spotted a plexiglassed corner of an upstairs nook, where my child's teacher sat calmly as the poor kid wailed and pushed against the wall, tears flowing down his little cheeks. I looked at her as I walked out, and she gave me a smile that said, "This is what we do."

As a parent, I am trying to learn the best ways to respond to these situations. One technique that I recognized the teacher using is to simply stay with the child when they are feeling the big feels, whether that be sadness, frustration, or anger. Instead of giving them a time-out, leaving them to calm down on their own, the idea is to simply stay with them, naming their feelings without shaming them for the serious emotions they are having. (I'll let you know in a decade if it works!)

It is not unlike what our churches are called to do. On any given day, many of us are dealing with various crises and losses. In the rest of life, the messages we get are basically, "Your feelings do not belong here. You need to get it together so the people around you can be comfortable." And so we take our time-outs, crying alone in our rooms or lashing out at our loved ones or settling into our addictions.

The church can be a unique community in our lives where we can bring our whole selves, including our big feelings. Good Friday is an especially good opportunity for this. The story ends in the tomb. And, lest we spoil Easter Sunday, we cannot put a happy spin on it. It is an uncomfortable opportunity, in our preaching and our worship acts, to sit with that story of Jesus and with the real life hard feelings of our communities without any shame, allowing the tears to run and the wails to be heard.

Secondary Preaching Themes

Many of us have grown up being taught that the significance of the crucifixion of Jesus is that it was a singular event with a singular meaning: that Jesus died in our place because God requires some kind of payment for our sins. Because many in your community probably grew up with this same narrative, if you have found new ways to reframe the crucifixion of Jesus, I would encourage you to name the normative account and then to complicate it with your own understanding.

Over the years, it has become important to me that Jesus's crucifixion was actually not a singular event, but that it is and was a common event. In Jesus's own time, crucifixion, torture, and violent militant intimidation were common ways of terrorizing the colonized public into both complicity and rebellion. Today, we find resonances with Christ's death everywhere—from the domestic abuse of loved ones, to the exploitation and disappearance of undocumented immigrants from their communities, to the killing of unarmed black lives at the hands of the state, to our own everyday tragedies and injustices.

Exploring the words of Isaiah and Psalm 22 make this point well. These texts were, most scholars agree, written about people other than Jesus. Isaiah was written in a context of violent exile and oppression. The psalm was written by a very harmed and humiliated individual. For me, the crucifixion does not have to be a singular event; instead, its meaning is in how it illuminates and dramatizes the cruelty, injustice, and suffering in the lives of so many. How have you come to understand it?

Litany

My God! My God, why have you left me all alone?
Deliver me from this isolation.
My heart is like wax; it melts inside me.
Deliver me from this depression.
My strength is dried up. My tongue sticks to the roof of my mouth.
Deliver me from this sickness.
Dogs surround me; a pack of evil people circle me like a lion.
Deliver me from this humiliation.
Oh, my poor hands and feet! I can count all my bones!
Deliver me from this hunger, from this suffering, from this injustice.

Sending Forth

Go out into this terrible night.
Holding onto faith—
If your burdens are too heavy,
we can hold some extra faith for you—
Faith that our story does not end here.

April 12, 2020– Easter Sunday

Passages: Acts 10:34-43 or Jeremiah 31:1-6; Psalm 118:1-2, 14-24; Colossians 3:1-4; John 20:1-18 or Matthew 28:1-10

Mark A. Miller

Gathering Prayer

This past week, fear and hatred had done their very worst, despair had had its day. Sorrow and sadness were in the air, a gloom would not go away. But early on the first day of the week, Mary saw the Lord, and now we all can say Jesus is alive! The unending, unquenchable power of God's love has brought him back! Hallelujah! Amen!

Preaching Theme

Violent earthquakes, fearful friends, tearful disciples, running men, appearing angels, disappearing bodies, empty tombs, mistaken identities, more running, more tears and fears, running to and fro. Confusion, chaos, conflicting messages (stay here or go to Galilee?). Easter sounds more like a disaster story in desperate need of FEMA rather than the triumphant Jesus comeback we retell year after year.

We really don't want to go there on Easter Sunday. We much prefer the shiny golden cross, the trumpets, the happy hymns in major keys, the heavily perfumed Easter lilies. We deserve this after all we've been through. Holy Week nearly drove us off the rails; worship can't get more depressing than Maundy Thursday and Good Friday. We need an upper! A shot in the arm! A win for the team!

But if resurrection is really about new life, then it is messy, stressful, and emotional. It is most likely not without physical pain. I once heard a young preacher compare childbirth to the new life of Easter. "Jesus is NOT AN EPIDURAL!" he blurted out. What an inspired sentiment. We can't use Jesus to numb the pain of some new thing God is trying to show us.

Think about death-defying. That's what resurrection is. What activities use the term *death-defying*? Bungee-jumping off a mile-high cliff? Swimming with great white sharks? Death-defying is TERRIFYING. I'm not saying that we should turn Easter into an Evel Knievel/Halloween Holy-day, but there is something way too pretty about our packaging of Easter into egg hunts and chocolate crosses when the idea of life-death-resurrection should be unsettling and awe-inspiring in the truest sense of the word.

Of course, there is another side of new life. There are tears of deep joy and surprise, gratitude and wonder. How did this happen? How can this happen? The miracle of life continues to astound and confound us. Peace be with us.

Secondary Preaching Theme

Resurrection is about bodies. Jesus's ministry was a ministry of touch—healing touch. Mary's natural inclination was to hold him when she recognized him. And this was most likely his way as well, but he had to caution her,

"Do not hold on to me, for I have not yet ascended to the Father" (John 20:17 NIV).

Mary, one of the last people to see Jesus alive on the cross, present at the burial, and the first to see the empty tomb and see Jesus (or the gardener, as she supposed) is an incredible figure in the Gospels. Without her testimony to the life, death, and resurrection of Jesus Christ, we would not have had such a powerfully transforming narrative. Her witness is profoundly authentic and brings a "realness" to the Gospel resurrection stories.

Easter Prayer

We shout for joy, for surprise, for new life!
The stone the builders rejected
Has become the cornerstone.
God has done this, and it is marvelous in our eyes.
God has done it this very day;
Let us rejoice and be glad!

Benediction

Go from this place, in the name of a death-defying, fiercely loving savior, willing to tell the good news that love is stronger even than the power of the grave. Go from this place, realizing that like Mary, you too may not recognize the resurrected savior standing right in front of you. May our eyes be opened and our lives forever transformed by an encounter with the risen Christ.

Suggested Anthem

"I'm Back," words and music by Mark A. Miller. Published by Chorister's Guild, 2019.

April 19, 2020– Second Sunday of Easter

Passages: Acts 2:14a, 22-32; Psalm 16; 1 Peter 1:3-9; John 20:19-31

Christopher Heckert

Gathering Prayer

God of limitless and unbounded love, you came into our midst as one who overcame every boundary and barrier, even that of death. Move among us now as one who can speak healing through wounds, hope in despair, and faith despite our doubts. Breathe resurrection power in the dead places of our hearts, and strengthen our witness so that others may come to see because of what we have seen and heard. Amen.

Preaching Theme

Several miles outside of the city of what is today Chennai, India, lies a sacred memorial called the Saint Thomas Mount. It is the traditional place where Thomas the Disciple was martyred after having journeyed there to plant one of the early churches and spread the good news of Jesus Christ. The courage it took to journey so far from home and to sow seeds of the gospel in what is today southeastern India must have required great faith.

Doubt is often seen as the opposite of safe. But in John 20:19-31, we see that doubt can be a pathway that opens up and ultimately leads to great faith. Just one week after we celebrate the resurrection of Jesus, we are faced with the timeless story of "Doubting Thomas." Jesus appears to his disciples, and they get to see physical proof of his resurrection. Yet, later, when Thomas asks to see proof because he was not there when Jesus appeared the first time, he seems to be chastised by Jesus and, in our tradition, branded as a doubter.

If we look closer, particularly to the end of the passage, we see that in fact it is about the reader and not Thomas himself. Because, like Thomas, the reader will not have had a physical encounter with Jesus, nor will they have an exhaustive memoir of his life. What the reader has is the gospel, the story of the good news of God through the life, teaching, death, and resurrection of Jesus Christ. The reader or hearer of the gospel fills their faith because they believe without the need to see. Nobel Peace

Prize recipient and author Elie Wiesel famously spoke of his experience interviewing Holocaust survivors noting, "When you listen to a witness, you become a witness."

This Easter season, we are witnesses to the resurrection power of God's love.

Secondary Preaching Theme

In Acts 2, through Paul's message to the Israelites, we see that Jesus's living as Messiah goes beyond the traditional expectations of one who is to become a ruler. Messiah, or Mashiach in modern Jewish texts transliterated into English, is the one who is to be anointed with oil, which claims them to be the next king. Because Jesus overcame death, he is not like King David or other great monarchs before him but instead is one who brings salvation and redemption in a deeper way, greater than the people could have imagined. The resurrection is central in Jesus being the only one who can offer the salvation of souls and redeem the most wounded and broken parts of our humanity. Of this resurrection power, we are to be witnesses.

Call to Worship

Christ is Risen!
Christ is Risen, indeed!
Even when we struggle to see the good news in the face of poverty, injustice, conflict, and woundedness,
Christ is Risen, indeed!
Even when our hearts hurt and we struggle to find hope to get us through another day,
Christ is Risen, indeed!
Even when we are faithful and yet we see little proof of our labor,
Christ is Risen, indeed!
Glory be to God who has overcome death and gives us faith, hope, and love that overcome all things. Amen.

Benediction

Go and be a witness because of those who risked and journeyed, struggled and loved. Go and be a witness to what God's love can do in the world to overcome broken systems, strained relationships, and human greed. Go in the love, grace, and peace that God gives, and may we be the church in a hurting world. Amen.

April 26, 2020–
Third Sunday of Easter

Passages: Acts 2:14a, 36-41; Psalm 116: 1-4, 12-19; 1 Peter 1:17-23;
Luke 24:13-35

Jim Winkler

Gathering Prayer

God, you call us out of our fear and distress and into the light of a new day and a new hope. Through their encounter with the risen Christ, the apostles found their voice and proclaimed your truth even at the risk of their very lives. Let us never forget their commitment and courage. May we stand for the right of all people of faith to worship safely as they choose. For we know that we are truly free when all are free. Our faith should not be taken for granted. We have decided to follow Jesus. There is no turning back.

Preaching Theme

Acts 2:14a, 36-41, although used here on the third Sunday of Easter, is most often associated with the day of Pentecost. However, Pentecost is yet to be celebrated. Thus, we are provided with an interesting juxtaposition with the Lucan passage related to Emmaus.

The words of this passage come from the sermon/speech that Peter delivered in the midst of a crowd of stunned onlookers in Jerusalem, who had just heard a mighty wind and watched as tongues of fire rested on each of them. That diverse crowd of Jews and Gentiles gathered in the cosmopolitan city had felt the Holy Spirit come upon them and were given the gift of understanding each other's language, though foreign to them. Now, emboldened by that experience, Peter declares that the time has come for them to repent, be baptized, and follow the risen Lord.

What a contrast this scene is to the one painted in today's Gospel lesson. It is just a short time after Jesus's crucifixion and his disciples have fled out of fear for their own lives. The two we meet on the road to Emmaus are filled with doubt and fear, and it seems hard to believe that in just over a month's time these disciples would be boldly preaching a message of salvation and repentance. It is amazing what the Holy Spirit can do to give strength and voice to the powerless.

So we have this lesson to remind us that only a few weeks after Jesus has been executed by the military forces of the occupying superpower of Rome at the behest of influential local Jewish religious leaders, Peter and other followers of Christ are now emboldened, so much so that they are ready to place the entire Jesus movement at risk of annihilation.

It is not coincidence that it is on the streets of the very city where Jesus was killed that Peter boldly announces "this Christ who you crucified" is both Lord and Messiah. And it is in direct contrast to the mob that turned on Jesus during the week we call "Holy" that, out of this crowd, three thousand persons were added to the movement that day. Indeed, one wonders if some of the people in those two crowds were the same.

Our faith is at its most intense level when it is severely tested. There may be times when we find ourselves frozen by fear and unable to see that our present and future still belong to God. Yet if we can muster enough faith in the midst of our struggle, we might find our own voice to speak the truth to power.

Secondary Preaching Themes

In Luke 24:13-35, Jesus is dead and those who follow him are so distraught they utter those desperate words, "We had hoped…" But when they encounter the living Christ, they do not recognize him until he breaks bread with them. One of the most important, but oft overlooked lines in the text says, "They got up right then and returned to Jerusalem" (v. 33). And in that moment they are able to face their fears and claim their future—God's future. What does it mean to realize that in all the years that have passed, with all of the archeology and exploration that has taken place in that region, no one has ever found the location of the village called Emmaus, even though it was only "seven miles" from Jerusalem? Perhaps Emmaus is the place you go when you need to find hope.

The Psalms should always be read with emotion and intensity. Psalm 11:1-4, 12-19 is a message of sincere thanks to God for saving one from a desperate situation. I spoke recently with someone who narrowly escaped death. He felt he had a new lease on life thanks to God.

Responsive Reading (Based on Psalm 116:1-4, 12-19)

I love the Lord, because he has heard my voice and my supplications.
Because he inclined his ear to me, therefore I will call on him as long as I live.
What shall I return to the Lord for all his bounty to me?
I will lift up the cup of salvation and call on the name of the Lord.
I will pay my vows to the Lord in the presence of all his people.
O Lord, I am your servant; you have loosed my bonds.
In the courts of the house of the Lord, in your midst, O Jerusalem.
Praise the Lord!

Benediction

Easter people, raise your voices, for the fear of death can no more stop us from our pressing here below. For our Lord has empowered us to triumph over every foe. May the encounter we have had with the risen Christ give us strength to live as people who no longer fear death as we speak the truth to power and spread the good news of God's unfailing love. Go in peace and change the world.

May 3, 2020–
Fourth Sunday of Easter

Passages: Acts 2:42-47; Psalm 23; I Peter 2:19-25; John 10:1-10

Javier Viera

Gathering Prayer (Based on Psalm 23)

We often swim troubled waters, O Shepherd, yet you promise to lead us to still waters. We are often wearied and depleted by the challenges life presents, yet you promise to renew and restore our soul. You promise that though we walk haunted by the shadow of death, you comfort and guide us. We have gathered to worship, to give thanks, to learn how to trust that come what may, we will dwell with you forever.

Preaching Theme

In the reading from the Acts of the Apostles, we find a description of how the earliest Christians shared life. Were we to take this depiction of embodied faith seriously, it would likely challenge every aspect of our own lives and faith. Yet, idealizing it or dismissing it as a failed experiment in early Christian living fails to fully appreciate its practical and spiritual import for contemporary life and faith.

Five simple yet important characteristics are revealed in this brief text. First, "They devoted themselves to the apostles' teaching and fellowship." In other words, they were learners; they were a community of seekers who hungered to understand the breadth and depth of the mystery that is God.

Second, "They devoted themselves to the apostles' teaching and fellowship." Fellowship is not a separate activity; rather, it is an integral description of what it means to learn the way of Jesus. Christian faith and spirituality is not a solitary experience for it makes sense only when it is lived in relationship to others.

Third, they also devoted themselves "... to the breaking of bread and the prayers." As they learned about God and learned how to share life with one another, the early Christians were moved to worship. They paused to give thanks for their new knowledge and sought first to be in communion with God. They gave thanks by sharing the meal that united them to Jesus and to each other. This meal was the natural and only place to turn, and it was there that they offered prayers for themselves and for the world.

Fourth, "All who believed were together and had all things in common; they would sell their possessions and goods and distribute the proceeds to all, as any had need." This is the part that scares us, or that we dismiss too quickly. It scares us because we love our money and our things too much. We dismiss it by labeling it "socialist," "communist," or "idealist." The point, however, is that as the early Christians learned their faith, lived in relationship to one another, and worshipped God, they became generous people. They learned that you cannot faithfully follow the way of Jesus and not be extravagantly generous. Jesus gave all—literally all—for us. Generosity to the work of God and the work of love and justice in this world is as integral a part of the Christian way as attending worship, praying, and learning. Someone who spends a lot of time in prayer but is not generous has missed the point. Someone who says "I give my time" but doesn't give a dime has missed the point. The early Christians were extravagantly generous. As a matter of fact, in the earliest descriptions of them by non-Christians, it was their love and care for one another and their generosity to those in need that was most striking and compelling. Their generosity was their most powerful way of evangelizing or witnessing to their faith.

Last, as a result, "the Lord added to their number daily (Acts 2:47 NIV). They lived peacefully, shared their lives and resources, worshipped together daily, and they had glad and generous hearts and the goodwill of all the people. What an amazing legacy. And they were growing every day! That's an astonishing reality.

This description of a healthy, thriving church is the same description that we could provide for a healthy, thriving life. If you are a devoted learner of the ways of Jesus, if you share life with other learners, gather regularly around Jesus's table, give of your time and resources generously for the work of God and the welfare of God's people in need, chances are you are on the path to a healthy, thriving, fulfilling life.

Secondary Preaching Theme

First Peter 2:19-25 is yet another unsettling text for settled and comfortable people. The way of the cross is the way not just for Jesus himself, but for all those who claim to be his followers. Suffering is not something to be avoided but accepted as part of the reality of life. A characteristic of Jesus's followers, however, is how they transform or subvert that suffering and make it something generative and life-giving instead. Rather than allowing violence against us to turn us into violent or violence-accepting people, Jesus's followers transform that violence into a radical peacefulness and non-violent resistance. Suffering and violence impacts us all, but as Christians we embody an alternative ethic of suffering love after the example of our crucified God.

Call to Worship

The Lord is our shepherd,
who leads us to still waters.
The Lord is our shepherd,
who restores our soul
The Lord is our shepherd,

whose goodness and mercy shall be with us all the days of our lives.
Open our lips, O Shepherd,
and our mouths shall proclaim your praise.

Prayer following Sermon

Generous and loving God, you called your people to live in peaceable community regardless the cost, to share resources and to provide for the needs of all. We offer you now the fruits of our life's labors in the hope that it will provide sustenance for those in need, hope for those who despair, and opportunity for those who need a way forward. In our giving and in our living may your kin-dom of love and peace finally become a reality in our midst. Amen.

Benediction

My brothers, sisters, and siblings in Christ, our worship never ends; it must be lived. Go into the world determined to share your love, your wisdom, your resources, and your labors so that those who are in any need may see in you the face of Christ. Go in peace. Amen.

May 10, 2020– Fifth Sunday of Easter; Festival of the Christian Home; Mother's Day

Passages: Acts 7:55-60; Psalm 31:1-5; 15-26; 1 Peter 2:2-10; John 14:1-14

J. Terry Todd

Gathering Prayer

Risen Christ, our hearts are made glad by your love for us and for all your creation. As we gather in your name, kindle in us a desire to follow you more faithfully in the way that leads to truth and life. For we ask it in your blessed name. Amen.

Preaching Theme: A House With Rooms to Spare

Jesus offers a capacious vision of God's realm in the opening verses from today's Gospel reading. "Don't be troubled," he says, and then invites us to trust God's provision of a house with rooms to spare. Yet Jesus's words don't quite pierce the disciples' doubt and confusion. Speaking for the disciples and perhaps also for us, Thomas says, "Lord, we don't know where you're going. How can we know the way?" Jesus responds, "I am the way, the truth, and the life. No one comes to the Father except through me."

For some Christians Jesus's enigmatic response has become a charter for Christian exclusivism, scuttling the "house with rooms to spare" message of the earlier verses and substituting instead a simplistic declaration of belief as a litmus test for salvation. And salvation, in this understanding, often has little to do with life on *this* side of the grave.

In *Speaking Christian*, Marcus Borg leads us into a deeper consideration of what Jesus meant in John 14:6.[1] "Jesus incarnates, embodies, enfleshes what can be seen of God in human life. To say 'Jesus is the way, the truth, and the life' is to say, 'What we see in Jesus is the way, the truth, and the life.' It is not about knowing the word Jesus and believing in what is said about him that is 'the way.' Rather, the way is what we see in his life…" (173). Borg's interpretation turns the emphasis toward what Jesus taught and how he lived as the ultimate expression of God's revolutionary love for all people. The Risen One walks in the way of truth and life, and calls us to do the same. "I assure you that whoever believes in me will do the works that I do" (v. 12).

Secondary Preaching Themes: Rocks, Stones, and Spirit

As the church's calendar and its lectionary carry us inexorably toward Pentecost, it's important to note the presence of the Spirit in today's reading from Acts. The passage presents the harrowing account of the stoning of St. Stephen, considered to be the first Christian martyr. Stephen is emboldened by the Spirit to confront the powerful players of his day and their embedded idols and ideologies. He retells Israel's sacred stories from the vantage of the marginalized, and infuriates the authorities by declaring "the Most High does not live in houses built by human hands." (How many of us church folk would also be enraged by such a bold prophetic claim?) The anger of the powerful reaches a murderous crescendo when, "enabled by the Holy Spirit," Stephen has a vision of God wildly at odds with authorized versions. It costs him his life. Yet even as he lay dying, he asks for mercy for his tormentors, saying, "Lord, don't hold this sin against them."

The writer of the passage from 1 Peter similarly evokes the matter of God's dwelling place when telling the persecuted Christians in Asia Minor, "You yourselves are being built like living stones into a spiritual temple." The challenge that continues in our day is to experience *church* not so much as a stone and concrete building, but as a pulsing living temple made up of a "royal priesthood" who follow in Jesus's way.

Worship Helps

The African American spiritual "Plenty Good Room" (*Songs of Zion*, 99) amplifies the message of God's wide embrace and extravagant welcome. Like so many other spirituals, "Plenty Good Room" can be read as a hope for liberation in this life as well as in the heaven that awaits the saints after death. The song tells us there is "plenty good room in my Father's kingdom," reflecting a central teaching in today's Gospel reading, "My Father's house has room to spare." The generations who've sung "Plenty Good Room" are a people who've endured enslavement, Jim Crow apartheid, and continuing expressions of racist sentiment in our own time. The line "just choose your seat and sit down" is an expectation of heavenly realities, yet it is also an expression of hope for human flourishing in *this* life as well. The good news of God's wide embrace, the freedom of choosing one's seat and to sit down, is meant for us now as well as then. It's not "a dream deferred."[2]

Closing Prayer

Holy One, through the strength of your Spirit, grant us grace to follow boldly in the way of truth and life. As we proclaim the dawn of your reign of justice and peace, remind us of your promise that in God's house there is always plenty good room. In the fullness of time, draw all creatures into your loving embrace, for we ask it in the name of the One who was and is and is yet to come, Jesus the Christ. Amen

May 17, 2020–
Sixth Sunday of Easter

Passages: Acts 17:22-31; Psalm 66:8-20; I Peter 3:13-22; John 14:15-21

Jennifer and Todd Pick

Gathering Prayer

Author of Life, you gift us with breath, enfold us in love, and bless us with your presence. When we feel lost, remind us that you are always near. When you seem far away, show us that you are closer than our breathing. When we are lonely and afraid, send us your Companion to offer comfort and courage. Open our eyes, hearts, and spirits to recognize it's still Easter, and your unstoppable love abides with us always. Amen.

Preaching Theme

Have you ever tried to untangle a string of Christmas lights? It doesn't seem to matter how carefully you pack them away at the end of December, they always come out a year later in a big knotted mess. When we look at the relationships of love in this passage between disciples and teacher, parent and child, Companion/Advocate/ Spirit and keepers of the commandments, they become so intertwined with each other it is difficult to separate them. "On that day you will know that I am in my Father, you are in me, and I am in you. Whoever has my commandments and keeps them loves me" (John 14:20-21). Each relationship, a beautiful bright bulb, is impossibly entwined with the other "bulbs" in the strand. It is their intimate connection that brings light to the world.

Having lived into the fullness of resurrection for a season, we find ourselves eagerly anticipating Pentecost. This passage is a bridge-builder between two liturgical seasons as well as between two kinds of endings/beginnings. John 14 takes us back in time to Jesus's Farewell Discourses as he desperately tries to prepare his disciples for the events of the next three days. We look at this passage through the lens of a resurrected Christ about to leave again—this time not in death, but through ascension. In both of these leave-takings, the promises of Christ hold true: We will not be alone. We will not be orphaned. We are too entwined with our creator and the love that made us to be left to our own devices.

Jesus promises another Companion. "Companion" is how the Common English Bible translates the word *paraclete*. "Companion" connotes someone who stands at our side when life is hard and the ground beneath us is rocky. This word sounds much softer and more comforting than the creative, fiery, uncontrollable Spirit that rushes in on the wind at Pentecost. Perhaps that is how we move from the season of Easter to Pentecost—first with a gentle Spirit that comforts, feeds, heals, encourages, and above all, loves. That love is what makes the Companion recognizable. That love is what sweeps us off our feet. That love is Jesus's first condition. It is the connection in our jumble of lights. "If you love me . . ." then all the rest of it—the dying, the rising, the living again, the Companion—will be possible.

Secondary Preaching Themes

All the scriptures this week seem to have familial love at their heart. In the Acts narrative, Paul is introducing his audience to the "unknown God" that has been in their midst since the world began. We can hear echoes of the Gospel passage in Acts 17:28—"For 'in him we live and move and have our being . . .'" (NIV). Just as the Johannine Jesus promises his disciples that he will not leave them orphaned, this passage from Acts emphasizes that we are God's children. The dynamism of love that is found between parent and child cannot be contained in static idols of gold, silver, and stone. We bear the indelible image of our divine parent.

In Psalm 66, the relationship of love is being tested between God and God's people. The psalmist asks if we are still able to see God's love when fire and water threaten to overwhelm us. Are we still be able to sing praises to the one who made us out of love? First Peter also speaks of a time when the people of God will face difficulties. He is writing to remind his audience that we bear a resemblance to our maker. We should take care to reflect Christ's love so clearly that Christ becomes visible in us.

Call to Worship

Come close and listen!
The One who made heaven and earth sings a song of life!
Come close and listen!
The One who raises us from the dead sings a song of love!
Come close and listen!
The One who walks with us through fire and water sings a song of hope!
Alleluia! We join the eternal song of life, love, and hope.
Alleluia! God's song goes on and on!

Responsive Prayer

We are never alone because you are always with us, O living, loving God. You promise to walk with us, encouraging us in faith. You promise to send us a Companion, keeping us on your pathway of truth. You promise to live in us, abiding with us forever. After a season of resurrection, we are now ready to live into your promises. Let our lives more fully entwine with your life. Enfold our very being in your never-ending, never-failing love as you continue to call us to rise. Amen.

Benediction

Renewed by God's abiding presence,
We are sent to make God's presence known.
Resurrected by the grace Christ offers us,
We are sent to make grace visible.
Refreshed by the Spirit who breathes deeply within us,
We are sent to companion others on the journey.

May 24, 2020–Ascension Day

Passages: Acts 1:1-11; Psalm 47; Ephesians 1:15-23; Luke 24:44-53

Sheila Beckford

Gathering Prayer
(Based on Acts 1:1-11 and Ephesians 1:15-23)

God, like the disciples, we too are gazing and in awe of your ascension.
We lift our hands to praise you.
We lift hearts to be strangely warmed by you.
We bear our souls to be revived by you.
Grant us the power to be witnesses of your greatness. Amen.

Preaching Theme

As a child I attended The United Methodist Church and the Catholic church, and both lent to my understanding of who I am in Christ. However, it was the Catholic church where I learned of the Ascension of the Lord.

Forty days after the resurrection, after walking, talking, and breaking bread with a couple of his followers (Luke 24:13-33), after confirming his fulfillment of the scriptures (Mark 9:31), and giving further teachings to his followers, Jesus delivered his final commandment (Acts 1:4-5) and mandate (Acts 1:8) to his disciples, then ascended into heaven.

We gathered on the fortieth day of Easter, which is always a Thursday, and listened to the Ascension story as it was recited by the priest. I can recall these words: "Jesus left this earth to be in the heavenly presence of God."

These simple words and his vivid description of the Ascension story allowed me the opportunity to visualize myself, at a young age, being lifted up from this earth and ascending into the heavens, as if I were Jesus. However, as my faith matured, I understood the Ascension of the Lord to be more than a physical act; it is also a transformative spiritual mandate.

If you are a Methodist, then this date, May 24, has a special meaning. It is the commemorative date of when John Wesley's heart was "strangely warmed," or the day of his transformative spiritual ascension.

John Wesley struggled with the same plight as the disciples: a lack of faith. For some time, he gazed into the sky for the answers to fulfill his unbelief. However, as Martin Luther's sermon "Preface to the Romans" was recited, John Wesley's heart ascended into the presence of God. He writes,

> In the evening I went very unwillingly to a society in Aldersgate Street, where one was reading Luther's preface to the Epistle to the Romans. About a quarter before nine, while he was describing the change which God works in the heart through faith in Christ, I felt my heart strangely warmed. I felt I did trust in Christ, Christ alone, for salvation; and an assurance was given me that He had taken away my sins, even mine, and saved me from the law of sin and death.[3]

Not long after this experience did John Wesley begin to live out his transformative ascension. He was a witness of the faith, and through his life, he became a witness for Jesus throughout the ends of the earth.

Secondary Preaching Theme

The book of Ephesians is where the rubber hits the road. The author writes to the people of Ephesus, "Since I heard about your faith in the Lord Jesus and your love for all God's people, this is the reason that I don't stop giving thanks to God for you when I remember you in my prayers" (1:15-16).

When people are witnesses of the faith, it ought to be evident. Our lives must reflect the love of God. We see media coverage of Christian groups who agree with separating children from their parents, slashing funding to systems designed to take care of the elderly and impoverished, and defunding educational institutions. These are no examples of the transformative witness of Christ.

Unfortunately, many of our churches are not living under the power of the Holy Spirit; their gaze is focused on political and individualistic gains. We are witnessing a faith in party affiliation within our churches more than we are seeing the Spirit of love. People ought to observe the fullness of Christ within the body of Christ. They should be encouraged to live like the people of Ephesus, who were once divided, but now live in unity, fulfilling the call to ascend into the presence of God.

Call to Worship (Based on Psalm 47, Acts 1:1-11)

Clap your hands, all you people!
Shout joyfully to God with a joyous shout!
Clap your hands, all you people!
The Lord has ascended
Clap your hands, all you people!
For we have ascended

Clap your hands, all you people!
We have ascended through the transformative power of God. We are mandated to be witnesses of your power. It is with joy that we live a life that bears witness to your love for all of your people. We clap our hands and give you praise for you have given us unspeakable joy!

Prayer of Repentance (Based on Ephesians 1:15-23)

Our risen Lord, we confess that we have not used your transformative power to be witnesses of the faith. We admit that we have allowed our political affiliations and individual aspirations to guide our decisions and actions, thus opening the doors to inhumanity, immorality, and injustice. Flood our hearts with your Spirit and may we be the body of Christ in the fullness of Christ, who fills everything in every way! Amen!

May 31, 2020–The Meeting of Mary and Elizabeth

Passages: 1 Samuel 2:1-10; Psalm 113; Romans 12:9-16b; Luke 1:39-57

Editor's Note:
Two entries are present here for May 31, one focused on the celebration of Pentecost and another on the reminder of the meeting of Mary and Elizabeth. What does it mean to both remember the birth of God's church and the meeting of the two mothers whose sons would bear the gospel message—John the Baptist, and then Jesus.

Harriett Olson and Alisha Gordon

Gathering Prayer

To the God of Sarah, Hannah, Ruth, Mary, Elizabeth, and the countless women whose name we do not know and have not said, we ask for your divine power that rests within us to manifest itself in our lives today. Let the voices of those who carry your message of love be heard over the noise of division; let our stories of resilience and threads of commonality connect us to the power of the past, the beauty of the present, and the hope of the future. Amen.

Preaching Theme

The story of Mary and Elizabeth is one that reveals to us the power of intergenerational love and respect. Both women, divinely pregnant with sons, would find joy and respite in knowing there was someone else in the world who understood their experiences. It is through this kind of shared understanding, these connecting threads between people, that we better understand how God calls us to find the common threads in the most unexpected places.

I am reminded of a time during a spiritual growth retreat where a group of women of varying ages, some of whom knew each other, spent time sharing tidbits about their life within the group. Some named their favorite movie or number of siblings in their family. Others provided more intimate details about losing a spouse or a time when they experienced financial hardship. Whenever someone shared a piece of her story, another woman would chime in and say, "Me too!" Before the session ended, women found new connections with others that deepened and strengthened their relationship with each another.

We often face life feeling like we are the only one dealing with tough times. May we be reminded that through shared testimony we find connection and hope in knowing that we are not alone.

Secondary Preaching Theme

Again, we find the story of a woman whose divine encounter with God connects us to our own lived experiences with God. Both Hannah and Mary rejoice for not only what God has done for and through them, but for how God's mercy and kindness will dismantle systems of oppression and elevate justice. How can we begin to experience God's divine work in our lives as opportunities for transformation for others? Both Hannah and Mary's songs revel in God's divine timing, and they point their rejoicing toward how God will do great things for others. Too often we experience God's goodness and want to keep it for ourselves. But when we shift our perspective to see how what God has done for us will impact the lives of others, our receptiveness to divine the divine call grow.

Suggested Hymns

"The Song of Hannah," *Voices United: Hymn and Worship Book of the United Church of Canada*, 878"

"Canticle of the Turning," Lyrics and arrangement by Rory Cooney. (This could be sung before the gathering prayer in a lively, upbeat manner.)

"Canticle of Mary, (Magnificat)," *The United Methodist Hymnal*, 199.

Responsive Reading (Based on Psalm 113)

Praise the Lord! You who serve the Lord—praise! Praise the Lord's name!
We give thanks for the women whose obedience to their divine call changed the course of time for all.
From age to age, let the Lord's name be praised!
From age to age, the Lord God remembers our times of emptiness and joy and makes God's glory our covering.
Who could possibly compare to the Lord our God? God rules from on high; he has to come down to even see heaven and earth!
Who are we that God would be mindful of us? God calls us "friend" and in God we find our confidence to say yes to the impossible.

God remembers our cries and our laughter; God creates newness in our pain and in our time of rejoicing!
Praise the Lord!

Poetry Reading

"Celebration" by Mari Evans[4]

I will bring you a whole person
and you will bring me a whole person
and we will have us twice as much
of love and everything
I be bringing a whole heart
and while it do have nicks and
dents and scars,
that only make me lay it down
more careful-like
An' you be bringing a whole heart
a little chipped and rusty an'
sometime skip a beat but
still an' all you bringing polish too
and look like you intend
to make it shine
And we be bringing, each of us
the music of ourselves to wrap
the other in
Forgiving clarities
Soft as a choir's last
lingering note our
personal blend
I will be bringing you someone whole
and you will be bringing me someone whole
and we be twice as strong
and we be twice as true
and we will have twice as much
of love
and everything.

Benediction

God who empowers us to believe for the impossible, to pray for the invisible, to receive the intangible, let us go forth knowing that what you do through us has the power to change the world.

May 31, 2020–Pentecost Sunday

Passages: Acts 2:1-21; Psalm 104:24-34, 35b; 1 Corinthians 12:3b-13; John 20: 19-23

Tanya Linn Bennett

Focusing Prayer (from Psalm 104)

I will sing to God as long as I live;
as long as I am alive, I will sing.
Let my praise be pleasing to God.
I'm rejoicing in the Lord!

Preaching Theme

What to preach on Pentecost Sunday except from the Acts of the Apostles, Chapter 2. The rushing of wind and dancing of flames. The voices crying out in all the languages of the earth, and some that had yet to be spoken, heard for the very first time. Surprised and bewildered, the people gathered for the Feast of Weeks or Pentecost are astonished, even cynical. "They're filled with new wine," they cry, not recognizing the move of the Spirit to spring up something new among them. Peter cries out in the midst of the melee, "Now, this is what the prophet Joel was talking about, the wonders to occur in heaven with signs below, a day when the sun will be go shineless and the moon turned red." We have named this the birthday of the church, a day when everyone who calls on the name of God will be saved.

It seems we are in a time of new birth, rebirth, when labor pains have nearly overwhelmed us, stealing our energy and shaking our souls. Perhaps this is a time when Paul's words become more moving for us, these words from 1 Corinthians, reminding us that we can only build a church when we remember that it takes all of us, every one, being just what God has made us to be. We recognize what unifies us rather than divides us—our belief in the one God in three beings. As Paul names the spiritual gifts that may have been bestowed on us, we recognize them in ourselves or in the ones around us and affirm them as essential to the nature of the new church to become, becoming in a time that desperately needs this space of forgiveness, and belonging, and hope. There is no time to waste judging who is in or out, or who is more valuable or more honorable or more acceptable. There is no time for this now as there was no time for it when Paul wrote this plea to the church in Corinth. And, there's never time for it—it's not our place or task. As Paul reminds is, "Christ is just like the human body—a body is a unit and has many parts; and all the parts of the body are one body, even though there are many." In the spirit of that Pentecost Day, might we grasp onto the hope and promise that the prophesy has been made real, that the day has come when the church is rebirthed with joy and thanksgiving at all our diversity, all our difference, all our disagreement—where we find that the place we agree is in claiming the lifesaving love of Jesus Christ, expansive imagination of the Holy Spirit, and generous grace of God. The one agreement that keeps us in the Body, a Body that functions only because we are all present and contributing the gifts of the Spirit to the essence of the church—caring for the lonely, feeding the hungry, and sheltering the most vulnerable. Back to basics, no questions asked. If we were able to set aside our human instincts, acting only with the humility of the Jesus who calls us, might we be equally bewildered and amazed as those first Christians on that Pentecost day by the power and ingenuity of the creating Spirit?

Secondary Preaching Theme

Psalm 104 reminds us of God's immense creating power. As the earth has smoked with fire and volcanoes erupt and seas retreat as the earth burns up with the weight of human consumption and abuse, would we return to Psalm 104 and others like it to support a plea for justice for the planet and the universe? Does Psalm 104 and others like it compel us to new action and attention? As the psalm reminds us, when we turn our face from creation, God hides the holy face from us. Would God take God's breath away from us, as we have sucked the life out of nature, as the psalm suggests?

A Litany for an Unfinished Church

By Tanya Linn Bennett © 2010

> In 1968, the United Brethren and Methodist Church were joined together into the United Methodist Church. Dr. Albert C. Outler, theologian at Perkins Theological School best known perhaps for synthesizing John Wesley's approach to theology into the "Wesleyan Quadrilaterial," was the preacher of the hour. This litany for an "unfinished church," is based on Outler's reflection at that moment in the church's history, comparing it to the first church created by the Pentecost day.

We gather in this time and place, all of us from different times and places, here to worship God.

Many years ago, the people gathered and were ignited by passion for God, lit up by Pentecost fire, shouting out in Pentecost voices, carried away on Pentecost winds.

So many years later, we gather. We have learned new words, and written books of rules. We have heard the stories of our past. We come to create stories for the future.

We are an unfinished church.

Like those disciples so many years ago, we are not sure we know the way. We are afraid to make mistakes. We are afraid to fail.

We are an unfinished church.

But, Christ calls us to carry on the blessing of discipleship, to move forward in love and faithfulness, so that all might find a place in our holy space, our church.

We are an unfinished church.

So long as even one of us is left outside the door because of our cold heartedness, we are an unfinished church.

We are an unfinished church.

So long as any one is lonely, hungry, sick, in prison, naked, we are an unfinished church.

We are an unfinished church.

So long as any one of us is destitute of the great Hope that is our future in Christ Jesus, raised up to set us free from death into holy and everlasting life.

We are an unfinished church.

Every day is a new Pentecost, full of the promise and possibility that God offers.

Today is a day of dreaming. A Pentecost day filled with refining fire, and holy smoke, and winds of change, and voices full of passion for God and for each other.

We are an unfinished church, but we are God's church.

We are God's church, full of grace and love and hope. Today is a new Pentecost Day, may we be birthed again into new beginning.

Benediction

May we go out, honoring the Christ in each other, loving the Christ in each other, lifting up the Christ in each other. May we go in peace, one Body, now and always.

June 7, 2020–Trinity Sunday

Passages: Genesis 1:1-2, 4a; Psalm 8; 2 Corinthians 13:11-13;
Matthew 28:16-20

Gary Simpson

Gathering Prayer

We thank you that you are always with us no matter how high or low or far we may be. We pray today, dear Lord, that all of our Pentecost power has not fizzled out in the drudgeries of this week. Remind us today of where you met us, how you found us, and why you dared to even call us. May those remembrances today fire us again to be who you have called us in the world today and always. Amen.

Preaching Theme

Our Gospel text for today gives us opportunity to be reminded of the church's commission into the world. It is also a time to rehearse our belief about the essence of God.

On this Trinity Sunday, we find ourselves in the last gathering of the resurrected Christ with his disciples. Our Savior takes the disciples back to a familiar and mean-ingful place. They are brought back to the mountain where they were appointed. How their minds must have danced and their hearts fluttered with joy! It is both good and necessary to go back to the places that have helped define us. (How some of them may have altogether forgotten the place!)

But some things have changed. The resurrected Jesus now claims all authority belongs now to him in heaven and in earth. That is big. ALL. A.L.L.

It is enough to contemplate that kind of authority. Too often, such authority is sought and grabbed for by mortals, but Christ declares that it is his.

The word for power used here is not the usual word for power, *dunamis*, but rather *exouisa*. This distinction conveys the difference between "self-contained power" (*dunamis*) and "passed on power" (*exousia*).

One of the ways that Christ passes on this power to his disciples is through the commission of baptism. Profoundly and poignantly here, the risen Lord connects the ritual with the essence of God: "...in the name of the Father and of the Son and of the Holy Spirit."

Secondary Preaching Themes

The Second Corinthians passages lends itself to a concretized and tangible mani-
festation of the Trinity in the lives of the believers and a very simple framework for
the sermon: grace, love and fellowship. These three ought to always abide in the community of believers.

Call to Worship

O Saving God, you release your Spirit,
and we are amazed and puzzled by your power.
We hear the rush of a violent wind,
and we are stirred by your Holy Spirit.
We feel the heat of divided tongues of fire,
and we are brought to speech and made like one.
We speak Christ's story to the hungry world,
and we move with Christ to claim your peace.[1]

Benediction

*May we go forth, not in the strength of our own perceived power, but in the strength of the
One who created us, redeemed us, and sustains us, One in Three, almighty and everlasting. Amen.*

June 14, 2020

*Passages: Genesis 18:1-15 [21:1-7]; Psalm 116:1-2, 12-19; Romans 5:1-8;
Matthew 9:35–10:8*

Alisha Gordon

Gathering Prayer

*To the God who listens, as we gather today, let our listening originate not in our ears, but
in our hearts so that we may hear the true essence of your words. Remind us that you are
always listening, always hearing our heart's desires—and we trust that you will respond
in your divine time.*

Preaching Theme

There's no greater gift than to be listened to. I remember an elementary school
teacher always differentiating between "hearing" and "listening." Hearing is a biological experience; our ears hear sounds that are processed in our brains that foster and
further our understanding. Even when our biological hearing fails us, different aids
and apparatuses can assist us in hearing. But "listening" takes on a deeper process
where we bring our lived experienced into what we hear to find sympathy, empathy,
or common threads that connect what is said to a larger story.

In Psalm 116, the writer says that the Lord "hears [his] requests for mercy" and
"listens closely" to his cries. The psalmist has a confidence in God's listening capabili-
ties; there are many things the psalmist could name as the first of many actions God has
taken on his behalf, but it is the act of listening that he names first. Knowing that God
is not simply hearing, but listening to us, matters so much in a time when the voices of
the marginalized are often heard as inconvenient interruptions, like a mosquito buzzing
around one's ear. But the cries of the righteous pierce a part of our being that calls for us
to listen, to give attention to for the sake of both correction and action.

What resolve we have knowing that God listens to us.

Secondary Preaching Themes

Listen. Laugh. Joy. This sequence of events we find Sarah experiencing in Genesis 18:1-15 and again in Genesis 21:1-7 as she listened (more like eavesdropped) on

Abraham's conversation with three visitors to their tent. One of the visitors prophesied that Sarah would have a son within a year's time—and like we often do when we hear the unbelievable, Sarah chuckled to herself. Beyond her childbearing years, she listened and laughed at what seemed impossible—and would find herself listening, laughing, and *joyous* again in chapter 21 as the promises of God manifested themselves in a baby boy named Isaac, whose name, in fact, means "laughter." "Everyone who hears about it will laugh with me," Sarah proclaims.

There are times in our lives when we listen to the promises of God, whether through our own internal dialogue with the creator or through the mouths of those trusted pastoral advisors or a community of reliable others, and find ourselves laughing at the impossible. Both Psalm 116 and the Genesis text point toward the impact and reward of listening to God and hearing God's promises—even the ones that are impossible to believe. One thing is certain, as both Sarah and the psalmist learn, that God's promises are yes, amen, and full of joy.

Responsive Reading (Based on Psalm 116:1-2)

I love the Lord because he hears my requests for mercy.
My requests are sometimes loud, sometimes silent, sometimes frequent, sometimes irregular, but they come.
I'll call out to him as long as I live.
To what end will I stop calling on the Lord? For as long as I have breath, I will call on the Lord.
Because he listens closely to me.
Thanks be to God that God listens to me for when my mouth has no words to say, my heart speaks.

Benediction

As we go forth today, listen to God, self, and others for the Lord speaks through them all. Amen.

June 21, 2020

Passages: Genesis 21:8-21 or Psalm 13; Jeremiah 20:7-13 or Psalm
69:7-10, (11-15), 16-18; Romans 6:1b-11; Matthew 10:24-39

Grant Hagiya

Gathering Prayer (from Psalm 13)

Look at me!
  Answer me, Lord my God!
Restore sight to my eyes!
  Otherwise, I'll sleep the sleep of death,

My foes will rejoice over my downfall.
But I have trusted in your faithful love.
  My heart will rejoice in your salvation.
Yes, I will sing to You because You have been good to me.

Preaching Theme

Running like a thread throughout the Matthew 10:24-39 passage is the evangelistic call to proclaim Jesus Christ as Savior and Lord. Jesus will not remain hidden away but will be brought out for all to see. So, when God whispers to us in the darkness, we need to shout it for all to hear from the rooftops. If we share and give testimony to the life-giving power of Jesus, we will be acknowledged before God; but if we deny or fail to speak of this testimony, we may be forgotten by God also.

Why are we so afraid of the "e" word—*evangelism?* Is it because we do not want to be seen as religious fanatics or fundamentalists? Is it because we believe that it will turn people off to us, and in the name of popularity we want people to like us? Is it because we simply forget to share our faith and what it means to us because we are so busy and consumed by the hecticness of modern life? Or is it because our faith is so lukewarm that it does not rise to the level of enough importance to share with others?

When we truly stop to think about it, as people of faith, God has given us everything, absolutely everything in life itself. Jesus, as the incarnation of God, was the very embodiment of this life and sacrificed his life so that we might truly live. If we have been given such a gift as life itself, should we not be willing to share the acknowledgment of this gift with everyone we meet?

Think for a moment of the biggest gift you have been given by someone else. It probably isn't a material object, for that only fades with time. For me, the biggest gifts have been relational and spiritual: the gift of time with loving family, the shared experiences that make life worth living, the gift of a lifelong marriage partner, children (although there are short moments when I question that giftedness!), and great friends. I believe all of these gifts ultimately come from God in Jesus Christ through the Holy Spirit. These gifts are of such magnitude the least I can do is tell others about such blessings.

This witnessing doesn't have be to preachy or dramatic. It simply needs to be sincere and authentic. We all need to find ways to share our faith in a way that has integrity for us. But the bottom line is that we must share it!

Secondary Preaching Themes

The Epistle text from Romans 6 provides the theological "why" of our evangelism and witnessing. Just as Jesus was raised from the dead by an all-loving God, so too in our baptism are we raised to new life in Christ. In this way, life means to be in the presence of and communion with God. Death means the absence of God and Christ in our lives. Eternal life means to be in the presence of God forever. Isn't this worth sharing with others?

In Psalm 13, the psalmist gives direct testimony to the same why. In "restoring sight" to our eyes we escape the death of the absence of God. In trusting God, our hearts will "rejoice in your salvation." We then have no recourse but to "sing to the LORD" or share the good news to all who will hear.

Call to Worship

Lord you call us today to proclaim your presence.
We shout your name from the rooftops!
We resist the temptation to remain silent.
We will share our belief in you!
We risk being seen as foolish by an unbelieving world.
We will be laughed at and mocked.
We dare to share our witness of the life you have given us.
From the fire in our hearts, with praise and thanksgiving, we join now in worship and lift your name on high.

Offertory Prayer

Gracious and loving God, accept now these material offerings as a symbol of our love for you. May they represent our commitment to feed the hungry, house the homeless, and encourage the lost and lonely. However, with these gifts may we also commit to share the good news with people we encounter and witness to this life you have given us. Trusting in your power to use all of these offerings for the building of your kin-dom on earth, we pray in Jesus's name. Amen.

Sending Forth

Let us leave this place renewed in our faith and life.
God feeds with the bread of life.
Do not hide your faith but share it with others.
Because God has been good to us, let us share this goodness with others.
May the love of God, joy of Jesus, and companionship of the Holy Spirit be with you now and always.
Amen.

June 28, 2020

Passages: Genesis 22:1-14 or Psalm 13; Jeremiah 28:5-9 or Psalm 89:1-4, 15-18; Romans 6:12-23; Matthew 10:40-42

Karyn L. Wiseman

Gathering Prayer

Holy God, into this space we enter to become more committed to discipleship and faith. Into this time we are gifted with an opportunity to express welcome and inclusion to all we meet. Into this world we move as disciples of Jesus to change the world through radical hospitality and love for our neighbors both near and far. Amen and Amen.

Preaching Theme

Mister Rogers famously sang, "Won't you be my neighbor?" to begin his television show years ago. He was a pastor, encourager, and educator of children. His work and life focused on being kind and inclusive. His work and life also were focused on teaching. He knew that children are our present and our future. He knew that welcoming a little child is the greatest gift we can give to the world.

Matthew's use of the phrase "little ones" may be about children, but it also may have meant his disciples, those new to the faith community, those young in their beliefs, or those at risk in the world. It was definitely about inviting others into the journey, taking care of their needs, and taking care of the least or "little ones." Jesus prepares his twelve disciples to go out into the world. The last part of this sending is our text for today and comes as a teaching moment after the Sermon on the Mount. *Welcome* is a pivotal word for this passage. In both the NIV and the NRSV translations, the word is used six times in the passage.

However, I have to be honest and say that *welcome* is not one of my favorite words as it is used in the church. For many, *welcome* is equated with simple tolerance of those different from themselves. To many who visit churches who claim to "welcome" them, there is a distinct level of distrust. Most marginalized persons much prefer a place that exhibits radical hospitality and full inclusion than mere "welcome." This is definitely not the sentiment that I hear when Jesus uses the word. He was instituting a practice of hospitality for his disciples on their mission of spreading the good news. If anyone welcomed one of them, they were indeed welcoming Jesus and, by extension, God the Creator. We can reclaim this word for the church by exhibiting the kind of *welcome* that Jesus is asking of us.

Secondary Preaching Themes

As this text is the final part of Jesus's teaching about his disciples being sent out to share the faith, we are once again reminded about the need to evangelize others. Unfortunately, the "e" word has taken on many negative connotations over the last few decades. A lot of people see evangelism as a loud, judgmental, and in-your-face practice. The word *evangelism* can bring about images of knocking on doors, asking if those inside have "found Jesus," or handing out tracts on street corners declaring the doom of those who do not follow Jesus. Still the need—yes, the imperative—to share the good news is part of our commission as disciples of Jesus. Sharing the ways we have been reconciled and forgiven by Christ is part of truly being a disciple. Many Christians are nervous about sharing their faith. The preacher on this day can preach about how we can evangelize by our words and our actions in profound ways. In uniting these two themes, we see that telling the story of our faith journey can bring lost ones into the welcoming arms of Jesus. This is a word many need to hear.

Call to Worship

Welcome to worship. Welcome to community. Welcome to a place of grace.
All are welcome here. All are invited to be part of the family of God.
Welcome to the Word. Welcome to the fellowship. Welcome to a place of love.
All are welcome here. All are invited to be part of the family of God.
Welcome to hope. Welcome to inclusion. Welcome to a place of peace.
All are welcome here. All are invited to be part of the family of God. Amen and Amen.

Prayer of Repentance

God of all, we confess to you that we have not reached out to the "little ones" of our world in the ways we should. We confess that we have not followed in your disciples' footsteps by sharing the good news with others as we should. We confess that we have left too many out in the cold and have not welcomed them as we should. Holy God, we repent of these errors and pledge to do better with the help of the Holy Spirit. We pledge to make our lives reflect the gospel of the risen Christ. Amen.

Benediction

God of welcome and grace, lead us to follow you more closely.
Empower us to be the disciples you call us to be.
Send us out to bring comfort and aid to those who are alone.
Guide us to the "little ones" who need your love.
Amen.

July 5, 2020

Passages: Genesis 24:34-38, 42-49, 58-67 or Psalm 45:10-17 or Song of Songs 2:8-13; Zechariah 9:9-12 or Psalm 145:8-14; Romans 7:15-25a; Matthew 11:16-19, 25-30

LaTrelle Easterling

Opening Prayer

Loving God, our souls long for you as a deer pants for water, as a dry oak seeks succor at the root. We come seeking a deeper knowing of you; a knowing that transcends intellect and human understanding. Your marvelous word has stirred our hearts, and we want to meditate upon and with you more intentionally. Free us from the shame of bearing ourselves to you fully; loose us from the confines of a safe relationship. As we worship you today, may we enter the holy of holies and plumb the naked truth of your word, your grace, and your love.

Preaching Theme

It hurts so deeply because we love so deeply. These words are uttered time and again in reference to the pain of separation. The words drip with truth and yet only scratch the surface of the anguish that accompanies separation from a beloved. When one reads letters between soldiers and their loves, the raw emotion and tenderness leap from the page. That is how the Song of Songs is often understood, a dialogue between two very intimate partners. Even when understood as allegory, the verses resist timidity. This kind of rapturous intimacy is often missing when we discuss our relationship with God. There is often a distance, a kind of stoic admiration from afar. And yet, our deepest longing is for intimacy with our creator; to know and be known at an intimate level. We speak so highly of mystics such as Julian of Norwich and Teresa of Avila, and yet we rarely engage the book most given to mystical interludes. Why do we run from it? Who taught us to remain distant from the one who is love and created us in love? What is sacrificed in not knowing God more deeply?

A female as protagonist is found only in Song of Songs. While controversial among some theologians, for those unafraid to engage, it can provide a critical perspective on gender equality and enlighten our understanding of gender roles and masculine normativity. What pathways does engaging a female voice open? In the wake of #MeToo and the deconstruction of unequal physical agency, especially among those marginalized in our society, how might this scripture inform and reform our social norms?

In our McLives we are often racing to get somewhere, racing to be on time for another meeting, racing to deliver our children to their practices before running laps is required for tardiness. In these fast-paced lives we often rush through what should be important interactions and thoughtful conversations. This includes our prayer lives. With the popularity of movies like *War Room*, the notion of a prayer closet has been reintroduced. The ancestors often spoke of tarrying in the spirit to "have a little talk with Jesus and tell him all about our troubles." The delight the author takes in seeing her beloved come near is borne of a deep longing to be in one another's presence. That level of joy is not birthed in quick exchanges. In our over-scheduled lives, is time with God on the calendar?

Secondary Preaching Theme

So often Christianity or religion in general is eschewed as being too demanding, placing a heavy burden upon believers. In some circles there is the thought that life as a Christian is too confining or restrictive. These criticisms are derived from a belief that old friends and familiar places will have to be sacrificed on the altar of piety. Yet the verses in Matthew 11:28-30 are the very antithesis of burden. The CEB reads, "My yoke is easy to bear, and my burden is light." The writer of Matthew informs the reader that humble submission to God actually brings freedom and a way to lighten the load. Unlike the yoke of oxen, which is heavy and conjures images of being forced to work hard in the heat of the day, the yoke of Christ is love and companionship. As the Lord's Prayer illustrates so beautifully, those who walk with Christ want for nothing. Do our lives witness to Christ as burden-bearer?

Responsive Reading (Based on Psalm 145)

We lift you up high, our God, the true king. We bless your name forever and always.
The Lord is merciful and compassionate, full of faithful love.
We join creation in giving thanks for your provision; we extol your majestic glory.
The Lord is merciful and compassionate, full of faithful love.
You have met our every need by your powerful hand; generation after generation has been fed and nourished.
The Lord is merciful and compassionate, full of faithful love.
Even when we stumble and fall you lift us and secure our feet in a safe place.
We will tell of your righteousness and faithful love to our children and our children's children. Your praise will forever be on our lips!

Benediction

May the One who sees us as we are and loves us deeply still, loose you from your fear of vulnerable intimacy with God so that you may also more purely love one another.

July 12, 2020

Passages: Genesis 25:19-34; Psalm 119:105-112; Isaiah 55:10-13;
Romans 8:1-11; Matthew 13:1-9, 18-23

Laurie Zelman

Gathering Prayer

Gather us, Lord, from our scattered places, bring us here and help us to be truly present,
that your presence might proclaim itself to us, and we might receive your word. Amen.

Preaching Theme

In the CEB translation, Jesus's story that I knew as the parable of the Sower is retitled the parable of the Soils. The switch in emphasis is important; the focus on the sower tends to draw our thoughts to the one who is spreading the Word and leads me to think of flinging the word generously, knowing that much seed is not destined to flourish and yield a harvest. The parable of the Soils has us focus on the ground that will receive the Word. God gives the growth, but how do we go about preparing the ground to give the best chance for seeds to sprout and roots grow deep? As a gardener, I am long familiar with the perplexing fact that one year the tomatoes or peppers or berries will do wonderfully, the next year poorly. The soil is the same, more or less, as we humans are basically made of the same physical and psychic raw material. To prepare we must do what we can, working with the elements that are naturally there and allowing God to bring the growth.

How do we prepare the soil to be fertile? If we turn to literal gardening for inspiration, we find that soil is enriched by composting, that is, returning the by-products of what nourishes us back to the ground: peelings, carrot tops, coffee grounds, and the like. In other words, nothing is really wasted; all adds to the readiness of the soil to be a fertile place for seed. If we apply Jesus's metaphor to our lives, what looks like wasted time—time for reflection, for quiet, time away from screens, time just talking with a friend or stranger, time looking at the trees against the sky or the faces on the bus—all adds to the soil that makes us ready places for the Word to take root, grow deep, and be watered with the Spirit. We also work the soil, get our hands into it, pull weeds, break up hard clods of earth. This extended metaphor can be worked until it yields a growing, living understanding of the Word.

Secondary Preaching Theme

Jesus's metaphor compares the life-giving Word of God to seeds. Isaiah's words evoke the water cycle. We are aware of lakes and oceans, of the clouds forming, of rain falling and evaporating, and how that nourishes earth's life. For me, the understanding that much of the world's water is actually in the form of ice was a little less familiar. The earth stores much of her water. Preaching might explore cycles in the perception of the God's word and link these perceptions to historical themes. The different forms God's word may take, such as faith in action, protest, music, art forms, and styles of worship, could be linked to the different forms water takes and the way that the Word "...does not return to God empty, but accomplishes what God intends" (v. 11 paraphrase).

Prayer of Confession

Let me yield my life, let me feel the seed,
Of your awesome word taking root in me,
Jesus, Let my life be deep rich ground,
Do a work in me, Let your truth abound.
Help me overcome all my shallowness,
Where I'm hard as stone help me to confess.
Where I need to change, where I'm chained and bound,
Do a work in me, let your truth abound.[1] *Amen.*

Benediction

May we nurture the seeds planted within us, may we go out celebrating the life God gives us, may we carry the knowledge that life is precious and God is life-giving to a world that needs God's growth! Go with God!

July 19, 2020

Passages: Genesis 28:10-19a; Psalm 139:1-12, 23-24; Romans 8:12-25; Matthew 13:24-30, 36-43

Grace Pak

Gathering Prayer

Gracious and loving God, we gathered to acknowledge you as our God and to praise your name in all the earth. In our worship, reveal and make yourself known among us that you are no longer the God that we heard of but the God who is real and as close to us as our breath. May we know you so that we can make you known in the world through what we say and do. We pray in Jesus's name. Amen.

Preaching Theme

Jacob is a scoundrel who cheated the birthright and blessing out of his brother Esau. He is running away to save his life from his brother's anger. Jacob is all alone, vulnerable with an indeterminate future. He stopped at a certain place for the night. There is no shelter. He sidles up to a stone and falls asleep. And here, Jacob has a dream that would be a game changer.

Here, in this lonely, wild, and vulnerable place, God came to Jacob; and Jacob came to know God firsthand. This is a game changer because he has been hearing about God all his life from his grandfather Abraham and his father Isaac but never felt that God was real. Now Jacob knows God is real. Now Jacob is able to identify with God, not just as his grandfather's God and his father's God, but also as God of Jacob.

Moreover, Jacob knows that God is for him. This gracious God does not judge or chastise but meets Jacob where he is and gives him the promise of a future in spite of who he is and what he has done. God shows faithfulness by extending the promises made to Abraham and Isaac to Jacob. There are eight items in the promise; the first four pertain to the future generation, and the last four to Jacob. For a fugitive with an uncertain future, the promise of so many descendants like the dust of the earth, with land to live on, and a plan to bless every family of the earth, changes the whole outlook. Jacob knows for sure that there is a future for him. For an absconder who is so alone, the assurance that God to be with him, protect him, and bring him back and fulfill everything God promised lets Jacob know that he is not alone and will never be alone. God gives Jacob a future with the promise of posterity and addresses his immediate concerns.

When Jacob awoke from his sleep, he deems the place sacred because he encountered God. He set up the stone that accompanied him through the night as a sacred pillar and poured oil on it as a memorial to his God-experience. The stone was a reminder for himself and a witness to others that God is real. The mundane and ordinary rock becomes a sacred symbol and the mundane and ordinary place becomes "Bethel"—meaning "the house of God."

Secondary Preaching Theme

Reminiscent of the creation story where God created the world and it was good until the serpent tempted Adam and Eve to disobey God, the landowner plants good seeds but the enemy comes and plants weeds in Matthew 13. Jesus explains, "The one who plants good seed is the Human One. The field is the world. And the good seeds are the followers of the kingdom. But the weeds are the followers of the evil one" (vv. 37-38). Servants are not allowed to pull up the weeds lest they might pull the good wheat. Both wheat and weeds are allowed to grow side by side until the harvest. At harvest, wheat and weeds are separated by their fruit: the ripe golden wheat or the lack of it. The wheat separates the followers of the kingdom from the followers of the evil one. The golden grain feeds the hungry and nurtures life. The wheat provide sustenance and nutrition. The followers of the kingdom are a source of blessing for the world.

In what ways, does your life feed, sustain, and nurture others? What is one thing you can do today to be a source of blessing to others?

Offering Invitation

As followers of Christ, we are the wheat Jesus planted in the world to bear fruit that will sustain and nourish others. One of the ways we bear fruit is through our offering to the Lord for the sake of ministry. Let us give generously so that hungry are fed, needs are met, and Christ's love is shared.

Sending Forth

May the grace of our Lord Jesus Christ who came to make God real for us,
And the unchanging love of God who finds us in time of our deepest needs,
And the abiding presence of the Holy Spirit be with you in your continued journey. Amen.

July 26, 2020

Passages: Genesis 29:15-28 or Psalm 105:1-11, 45b or Psalm 128;
1 Kings 3:5-12 or Psalm 119:129-136; Romans 8:26-39;
Matthew 13:31-33, 44-52

Heather Murray Elkins

Gathering Prayer

Wise and Steadfast Guardian, gather us in.
Let us come before you in faithfulness.
May we bring upright hearts and open hands.
Give us an understanding mind to govern ourselves
in our nation, our neighborhood, our home, and our selves.

Preaching Theme

This Romans passage is a love song. It's actually a duet, sung by Paul along with the Spirit for the beloved community of Jesus the Christ. We might even consider it as the Holy One's poetic question and answer: "How do I love thee . . . let me count the ways." This would seem to be an easy task and text to preach. We know how well we have been loved by God in Christ. We also know that we are to love others as we have been loved.

The problem with preaching and practicing this text is that we get stuck or tongue-tied. Our language and the actions get habituated so that all the tender and truthful possibilities of expression get averaged and simplified. When called to express or vouchsafe our love in all its poetic possibilities, we often respond "ditto." The second problem we encounter is that when faced with the difficulties of all that does separate, distance, and alienate us from our love, we hit a barricade. We cannot cross, by our own will, all that divides us from those we love or love us, and this includes God. We are stopped at the barricade of suffering or sin and fall silent. There are no words for the crossing.

If we understand these difficulties of articulating authentic human experience, what can we say that would help us to name what we can't describe? God knows the bland and stuttering attempts we make to express and experience the mystery of love. God knows and has provided a way out of the boring and pretentious ways we express and experience this most real of all reality. God has given us the Spirit, who, as Paul reminds us, helps us through interceding, searching, and showing us how to say and do more and differently what the deep things we feel and know of the love of God. With the Spirit's help we turn our groans into songs of love.

With and within the Spirit, we don't need a focus group to test and market expression of our profoundest love. With the Spirit we need not depend on the traditions or accents of party or politics to bring love and justice to those who need it. The Spirit will take our stuttering ways and make us into holy human flesh. This is the beginning of the gospel of Jesus Christ, the beginning that will be completed in us. And as the prayer of Christ's table reminds us, "And so, with your people on earth and all the company of heaven we praise your name and join their unending hymn. . . ."

Secondary Preaching Theme

There is one theological problem with this passage that can also intersect with the 1 Kings text: the question of election. John and Charles Wesley parted company with George Whitfield over predestination/election. If predestination is understood as a justification for status quo or a facile condemnation of those who do not seem to have the right stuff/spirit, this is not what Paul meant. Wesley understood election as God calling special people for certain tasks, such as the way Solomon is offered the gift of leadership; it is not his DNA but the divine call on his life. The call of God that confirms, the purpose that conforms, the justification that glorifies is not something that is inevitable. It is the recognition of prevenient and amazing grace that cuts through the depravations and divisions that would appear to make the love of God and neighbor impossible. Solomon asks for wisdom, an understanding heart, and the ability to discern between good and evil. Freedom of will is part of who we are as humans, and we must choose to accept and express the love of the One who first loved us. Nothing can separate us unless we insist on separation and reject the love of God with our last breath.

Call to Worship

Come and help us, Holy One
We are like children who are lost.
Answer us, O God.
It is hard to hope for what we don't see.

Come and help us, Holy One
We are like children who are hungry.
Teach us wait with patience,
and to pray without fear.

Come and help us, Holy One
We are like children who are hurt.
Search our hearts for the words we can't say
And shelter, strengthen, heal our brokenness each day

Blessing/Charge

May God who is good all the time
work all things together for good for you who love God.
And for you who want to love God more,
God will work all things together for good.
And may you work for good for God's sake,
for those who do not yet know the love of our good God.
Amen.

August 2, 2020

Passages: Genesis 32:22-31; Isaiah 55:1-5; Romans 9:1-5; Matthew 14:13-21

Sudarshana Devadhar

Gathering Prayer

Compassionate God, may your abundant grace and mercy flow upon us, so we may truly encounter you in this hour of worship. Breathe upon us the fresh winds of the Holy Spirit, so our minds may be open, our hearts warmed, and our souls stirred to the love of Christ in a new way. We ask this in the precious name of our Lord and Savior, Jesus Christ. Amen.

Preaching Themes

Large numbers of people, some of them sick, followed Jesus on foot from the cities to a deserted place to which Jesus had gone to be by himself. When he saw the crowd, Jesus "had compassion for them and healed those who were sick" (Matt 14:14).

In the evening, the disciples urged Jesus to dismiss the crowd, so the people could go to the village to buy food for themselves, but Jesus told them, "There's no need to send them away. You give them something to eat" (v. 16). The disciples objected, "We have nothing here except five loaves of bread and two fish" (v. 17).

The disciples thought the resources they had were not sufficient. Jesus said, "Bring them here to me" (v. 18), and when Jesus blessed those meager resources, they were multiplied.

What are the implications of this powerful miracle for us as twenty-first century Christians? Numerous questions and preaching themes emerge from the text.

Compassion. What does it mean to be compassionate like Jesus? Jesus understood his crowd. He knew the needs of those who followed him. Do we understand the crowds around us? How well do we know the people in our own communities? How would our knowing them help bring healing?

Abundance vs. Scarcity. Do we, like Jesus's disciples, look at what resources we have and dismiss them saying they are not enough? Do we approach need with a sense of abundance or scarcity? When confronted with people with great needs, do we hope they will go away, or do we use what we have in order to do what we can to address the need?

Faithful Use of Resources. Do we sometimes dismiss people and the gifts they bring to ministry? I have heard Christians say that someone is not "good" for a certain church office because of all kinds of imagined reasons. Sometimes the person they are dismissing is simply different from them racially, culturally, or theologically. Such a loss to us, to them, to the church, and to the world!

Several other powerful sermons can be preached from this text: Who are the persons whose compassionate acts have made a difference in the lives of others? Another focus might be to look at the waste we create in our communities—and how to better share our natural resources, gifts, and personal possessions. Yet another sermon could be on stewardship challenging people to bring whatever they have to be used by God.

Secondary Preaching Themes

In Genesis 32:22-31, after his encounter with God, Jacob emerges with unbound blessings but also with a mark to remind him of those blessings for "[God] grabbed Jacob's thigh and tore a muscle in Jacob's thigh as he wrestled with him" (v. 25). Furthermore, because of this encounter, not only did Jacob get a new name, he also named the place Peniel (meaning "face of God") "because I've seen God face-to-face, and my life has been saved" (v. 30).

When was the last time we experienced God's unbound blessings? What are the marks of those blessings that we share with others? The prophet Isaiah (Isa 55:1-5) reminds the exiles who came from Babylon that salvation and abundant grace are free from God. Faithfulness to God's covenant comes from receiving this free gift of grace. As we do ministry and mission from the margins, what are we doing to ensure that everyone understands that people of all backgrounds can come at no cost and receive God's abundant grace?

Paul, who received and experienced God's grace and compassion in his life, said boldly, "I'm speaking the truth in Christ…" (Rom 9:1). The challenge for all of us is to share the true gospel—not a gospel of neutrality to please everyone or a sugar-coated gospel so we are popular. We must ask ourselves if we are "speaking the truth in Christ."

Unison Benediction

May we go forth as true disciples of Christ,
so others see the compassion of Christ in us.
May we share freely the marks of our encounters with God;
May we invite all people to God's table of abundance;
May we courageously speak the "truth in Christ";
May we go forth—
to glorify the God of creation,
to adore the Christ in others,
and to be vehicles of the Holy Spirit. Amen.

August 9, 2020

Passages: Genesis 37:1-4, 12-28 or Psalm 105:1-6, 16-22, 45b;
1 Kings 19:9-18 or Psalm 85:8-13; Romans 10:5-15

Kathleen Stone

Gathering Prayer

Holy and gracious God, sometimes we forget that you are here with each and every person we seek to reach. Sometimes we forget that no matter what one undergoes in this life, through whatever trial or tribulation, you are there to redeem and reveal mercy and love and in that we hope. Right now. Right here. Amen.

Preaching Theme

Surprising. Shocking. Right here. Right now. The presence of love is shockingly and surprisingly present at all times and in all places. In a world that has made it harder and harder for each of us to be present in the moment...in a world that grabs us and makes of us something that needs stuff all the time...in a world and a consumer culture that is always hoping for some better place, some more satisfying life, some more significant work, some many-colored coat like that guy over there...where so many of us hope that one day everything and everyone will be at peace and surrounded by the best of goodness...Jesus says, right here, right now. In our vulnerabilities, our struggles, our taste of our own hopelessness the strong and faithful arm of God picks us up, right here, right now. It's not over there or over there. It's right here. It's in the jail cells, in the injustice, in the hopelessness, in the betrayals. It's right here. Right now. No matter what. And nothing can separate us from that—not others, not ourselves, not circumstances. Paul declares in Romans, "The Word is near you, on your lips and in your heart" (10:8 NRSV). But the journey is shocking and surprising.

Secondary Preaching Themes

Imagine the scene, the despair, the hopelessness, and what must have felt like godlessness to Joseph. Imagine having all your brothers conspire against you, throw you in a pit, and then sell you to slave traders. Yet, as Joseph lived his life, he found God wherever he was—whether it was in the king's house or in prison, in the pit or being sold into slavery, in a famine or in overseeing relief efforts. Somehow, it didn't ultimately matter that he was given a special coat by his father. What mattered was his acknowledgement and journey into his own heart, through his dreams and the conversations with whomever came along, whether a jailer, a baker, a king, or his brothers. Precisely through his dreams—through the quality of his personality that his brothers had made fun of—precisely in his dreams and in the interpretation of dreams, God worked miracles in Joseph's life and in the world around Joseph. But none of it was how Joseph, his brothers, the king of Egypt, or his father had pictured it. None of it. Surprising. Shocking. Right here. Right now.

With Peter, he had hoped to walk on water to Jesus, and it was precisely in his self-imposed test of his bravado and his resultant failure that he found Jesus to be the arms he needed. Surprising. Shocking. Right here. Right now.

God is near us, on our lips and in our heart. Like the ocean that comes to us in waves, yet is always there . . . or the wind in the trees that can blow soft and strong, or which is there but still . . . or like the feeling of the hot sun on your back, which comes up every day, clouds or not . . . or the air you breathe in and breathe out. It is as simple as that. God is. "It" is. The test is to reach for God's hand when you're sinking, to dream when no one else dreams, and to know that the entire power of a God of life, who wants goodness for you, but without the preconceived ideas about what that looks like, that God is right here in our hearts.

Experiential Worship Element

Spend time in worship, breathing.
Breathe in acknowledging the holy.
Breathe out acknowledging the holy.
Breathe in acknowledging the holy.
Breathe out acknowledging the holy.

Carl Jung once said, "Bidden or unbidden, God is present." This quote could be given out on small bookmarks, or could be on seats/pews as people arrive, placed where they have to move the laminated or construction paper bookmark before they sit down.

Call to Worship

Let us pray: Gracious, Good God, as we gather ourselves this morning, help us to know that it is not over there or over there that you are found, but precisely here.
Right now. Right here.
In the middle of our lives, vulnerabilities, faithlessness, grief, and despair.
Right now. Right here.
In our praise, our hopefulness, expectation, and grace.

Right now. Right here.
No matter where we find ourselves, the Word we need is on our lips and in our hearts.
Thanks be to God.

Offertory Prayer

God, it is in the day to day, the everydayness that you are bringing forth the most extraordinary. We give of our everyday earnings because we know this. Because we know that without your love and presence, our lives would be so tiny, insignificant, full of many-colored coats where the status of privileged or imprisoned can defy dreams. With you we are held, challenged, gifted, and strengthened through the power of good times and bad times to hear your voice, in our hearts, in our dreams, right here and right now.

Benediction

We go out in the right here, right now to be the right people for just such a time as this. Amen.

August 16, 2020

*Passages: Genesis 45:1-15 or Psalm 133; Isaiah 56:1, 6-8 or Psalm 67;
Romans 11:1-2a, 29-32; Matthew 15:10-20, 21-28*

Jennifer and Todd Pick

Gathering Prayer

*Merciful God, your grace is bigger than we can imagine, wider than we can dream. In a
world where racism, hatred, bigotry, and fear diminish your image in others, you remind
us there are no exclusions from your family, no barriers to your open arms. Your expansive
welcome reminds us never to keep others from your life-changing love or deny them your
life-giving bread.*

Preaching Theme

There is nothing on earth as potent, tenacious, and determined as a mother
pleading on behalf of her child. Just a few steps into the region of Tyre and Sidon, a
mother cries out to Jesus to save her daughter. Having left the Galilee, Jesus travels
to the margins, to a liminal space where the land meets the Mediterranean. It's a
border where a Jew can meet a Canaanite. Unlike Mark, who identifies the woman
as Syrophoenician, Matthew recalls an ancient enemy of Israel: Canaan. This brings
centuries of history and conflict into the dialogue. No longer is it just a conversation
between a healer and one who wishes healing. It is about the indigenous people of
Canaan and their displacement by the Hebrews at God's command. Into this legend-
ary fray, a mother's voice can be heard calling Jesus by his Jewish messianic title, "Son
of David." By using this title, she implicitly acknowledges the priority of the Jews
in the divine plan of salvation. Jesus, however, does not respond to her; the ancient
borders are still firmly drawn. And yet this mother will not give up. She will cross
boundaries of animosity and cultural mores to save her daughter from the demons
that bind her. Approaching Jesus a second time, she assumes a posture of desperate
submission as she kneels before him and once again asks for help.

The response from Jesus is shocking to modern Christian ears: "It is not fair
to take the children's food and throw it to the dogs" (NRSV). This is not the inclusive, open Jesus we know who eats with sinners, forgives the unforgivable, and heals
the unworthy. It is not the Jesus who commands us to love our neighbors and our
enemies as ourselves. This is not the Jesus who, in a few short verses, will feed a crowd

of four thousand out of compassion. This rather rude Jesus is not the Jesus this Canaanite mother was expecting to find. So she challenges back, "Sir, even the dogs under the table eat the children's crumbs." She is not asking for a place at the table, only to partake in a small fraction of the feast—the leftovers forgotten beneath it. Her plea reminds Jesus that he should be about conquering human exclusions and the walls erected that separate God's children. Her cry opens him to respond to her faith. And in this openness the kin-dom widens, allowing Jesus to call others to be open as well.

Secondary Preaching Themes

Themes of eventual divine inclusion and reconciliation are prominent. In the Genesis narrative, Joseph affectionately welcomes his brothers who sold him into slavery. Even though they acted with hatred in the past, God ultimately brings about a joyful family reunion with forgiveness and reconciliation, where former divisions come tumbling down. Similarly, in Paul's letter to the Romans, reconciliation and inclusion are achieved by the equality found in and the universal need for God's mercy.

In Genesis, Romans, and Matthew, there is the loud question of God's faithfulness to Israel. The answer that echoes indirectly from all three texts is that God's faithfulness to Israel is not predicated on the exclusion of other peoples from divine salvation. These scriptures show us God's *kin-dom* is wide enough for all.

Call to Worship

Like doors open wide, welcoming all who gather here,
God's hands are outstretched, extending mercy to all.
Like many grains brought together in one loaf,
God's love binds us as one, making us living grace for all.
Like a persistent mother refusing to be dismissed or denied,
God's voice cries out, calling us to justice and right relationship with all.
Like a party for the outcast, the foreigner, and the stranger,
God's heart gathers us into a joyful house of prayer for all.
Let us worship God, whose love is for all!

Litany of Repentance

Welcoming God, open our ears to the cries of the oppressed and the outcast.
Open our eyes to recognize you in the weary and the wounded.
Open us, we pray.
Open our hands to offer mercy to the desperate and the distressed.
Open our hearts to risk loving the least and the lost.
Open us, we pray.
Open our mouths to speak life-giving words of healing and hope.

Open our tables to offer bread to the hungry and the hurt.
Open us, we pray.
Open our sanctuaries to welcome the stranger and the suffering.
Open our lives to your Spirit, who declares all beautiful and beloved.
Open us, we pray. Open us today.
And in our openness, reveal to us your reign of justice and joy.

Benediction

And now it is time for us to go and make Christ's love visible in the world.
We go as agents of mercy, singing Love's promise.
We go with arms open wide, extending Love's welcome.
We go with more than crumbs, but filled by a table of grace, dancing Love's invitation.
We go as living bread and living sign, sharing Love's story.

August 23, 2020

Passages: Exodus 1:8–2:10 or Psalm 124; Isaiah 51:1-6 or Psalm 138;
Romans 12:1-8; Matthew 16:13-20

Drew Dyson

Gathering Prayer

Gracious God, you have gathered us here as your church, united in love for you and love
for your children. Dwell with us now as we worship your holy name. Bind us together in
love that we may embody your love in our life together. Send us forth in love that we may
bear witness to your love in the world. Amen.

Preaching Theme

In our highly individualized culture, it is easy to look at this passage in Matthew's Gospel through the lens of Peter and to affirm Peter's faith as one who "truly gets it." Matthew's intent, however, is not to highlight Peter as a "Super Disciple," but to elucidate the work of Christ in building the church. Rather than a sermon asking individuals Jesus's powerful question, "Who do you say that I am?," what would it look like to preach a sermon that affirms the church and calls the church to the ministry of "binding and loosing"?

The true miracle of this story is not that Peter, the ever-impetuous one, dramatically identifies Jesus as the Messiah, but that Jesus would choose Peter as the foundation for building his church. In Matthew's Gospel, the disciples have already identified Jesus as Messiah, thereby limiting the drama of Peter's confession. The turning point of the story is rather that Jesus would build his church on the cracked foundation of a flawed disciple. What a powerful witness to the church that could open up a powerful moment in a congregation's life! In preaching this story, build upon Jesus's promise to Peter and his use of a flawed disciple as the cornerstone to build his church.

Jesus not only builds the church upon "the Rock," but also promises that nothing will prevail against it. For Matthew, the church was engaged in a cosmic struggle between the "gates of Hades" and the new kingdom that Jesus proclaimed. In our culture, the church continues to struggle against forces and powers of evil—from within and from without. The promise of Jesus, however, is that those forces will not prevail and that the church will stand.

The story doesn't simply end triumphantly, however, but with a charge for the church to live according to this new kingdom. The church is not to simply stand in victory but is given the power "to bind and to loose," perhaps unleashing the power of forgiveness and grace in the world or heralding the prophetic role of the church in fighting oppression.

Secondary Preaching Theme

The beginning of the twelfth chapter of Romans offers an opportunity to preach a sermon that ties together an invitation to personal faith with a powerful reflection on the nature and witness of the church. Paul begins this pericope with a powerful appeal for people to offer their whole selves to God as an act of worship. The passage continues, at the same time, with a powerful reminder that all of our "bodies" offered to God are knit together in "one body," with many gifts and each having importance in the life of the church.

This sermon is an opportunity for faith-sharing, inviting testimonies offered by folks who have offered their whole selves to God and who reflect on their role in the life of the church. As pastor, your role is to knit the stories together into a seamless whole, powerfully illustrating the work of the Holy Spirit in building the church with different gifts. There are powerful ways to visually illustrate this message—whether building a puzzle or creating a tapestry or web of life of sorts by passing a ball of yarn throughout a gathering with each person holding their strands—that will underscore the importance of individual sacrifice and communal witness.

Call to Worship (Based on Psalm 138)

I give thanks to you with all my heart, Lord.
I sing your praise before all others gods.
I bow toward your holy temple and give thanks for your loyal love and faithfulness.
because you have made your name and word greater than everything else.
Whenever I am in deep trouble, you make me live again;
You send your power to save me with your strong hand.
The Lord will do all this for my sake.
Your faithful love lasts forever, Lord!

Benediction

I am the church. You are the church. We are the church together! Go, church of God, into the world, that we might live as one and others will know us by our love. Go, church of God, into the world, that we might set loose forgiveness and grace and hope. Go, church of God, into the world, that we might proclaim the mighty works of God in our living and our loving. And as you go, may the love of God, the grace of the Lord Jesus Christ, and the fellowship of the Holy Spirit be with you always. Go in peace and may the peace of God go with you.

August 30, 2020

Passages: Exodus 3:1-15 or Psalm 105:1-6, 23-26, 45b; Jeremiah 15:15-21; Psalm 26:1-8; Romans 12:9-21; Matthew 16:21-28

Jim Winkler

Gathering Prayer (Based on Psalm 105)

Sing to God;
  sing praises to the Lord;
  dwell on all his wondrous works!
Give praise to God's holy name!
  Let the hearts rejoice of all those seeking the Lord!

Preaching Theme

Exodus is often viewed as the book that contains the saga of Moses, but the very title of the book is a reminder that it is really the story of one of the two most defining events in the First Testament—the Exodus and later the Exile. From here on, the worship life of the people will be defined by the phrase, "Remember, you were once slaves in the land of Egypt...." Exodus 3 focuses on the call of Moses by God, who has heard the suffering cries of the Hebrew people and has selected Moses to be the one to lead them out of bondage.

Moses seems an unlikely candidate despite his upbringing in the pharaoh of Egypt's household. Years before, when the Hebrews were growing in number and were perceived as a threat by the Egyptians, Pharaoh had ordered the infanticide of a generation of their male children. Moses had been saved from death by his mother, who put him in a basket and floated him down the river, where he was discovered by a daughter of Pharaoh who raised him as her own son. As an adult, Moses kills an Egyptian who was beating a Hebrew—one of his kinsman—and flees for his life. What a conflict this must have been for Moses! Raised as an Egyptian, he kills one of them in defense of a fellow Israelite. He becomes a refugee in the land of Midian, located in what is now western Saudi Arabia. And it is there while tending the flock of his father-in-law that Moses is called by God, out of a burning bush, to return to Egypt and free his kinfolk, the Israelites. Just as he was once rescued, now he is to be the rescuer.

Moses is directed by God to lead a liberation movement, to go into the very halls of power and demand freedom for his people, now slaves. Not only must he do so at the risk of his own life, he has to convince the Israelites to give him support. Those to be liberated must be active participants in the drama. This is a reminder to all of us that our faith is not a spectator sport.

We like to think that some people are called to extraordinary acts of courage, even to suffer for Christ (Martin Luther King Jr. or Mother Teresa or Dorothy Day, for example) and the rest of us have the duty to cheer them on and support them. But the Bible paints a different picture. We may never be called to lead a liberation movement, but everybody is expected to participate in God's plan. Everybody.

Secondary Preaching Theme

Our faith has been purchased at great cost. In Matthew 16, Jesus has just revealed to the disciples that he is indeed the Messiah and that he must face death and resurrection. Imagine the turmoil this causes among them. Peter goes so far as to rebuke Jesus, an act for which Jesus denounces the spirit of Satan within Peter. Can there be people upon whom we have placed our own hopes and dreams to such an extent that we have lost sight of the bigger picture?

Call to Worship

Remember, you were once held in bondage, enslaved and oppressed.
We remember.
Remember, the Lord our God has chosen us to be a people blessed to be a blessing to the nations.
We remember.
Remember, you were once strangers, living in a foreign land.
We remember.
Let us worship the Lord our God.
We worship God with all our heart, soul, mind, and strength.

Benediction

May the God who does not call the equipped, but equips the called, strengthen us for the days that lie ahead. Let us be active participants in our own liberation from false comfort, from slavery to sin and death, so that we, too, will be unafraid to speak truth in the halls of power.

September 6, 2020

Passages: Exodus 12:1-14; Psalm 149; Ezekiel 33:7-11 or Psalm 119:33-40;
Romans 13:8-14; Matthew 18:15-20

Vicki Flippin

Gathering Prayer

God, awaken my heart to the dawning of your revolutionary day—a day of justice and joy, a day of peace and repair. And especially when the night is most dim, give me friends to huddle in the dark with me, to face the horizon together, and to remind one another that the sun is about to rise. Amen.

Preaching Theme

This week's passage from Romans contains some of those early Christian beliefs about the second coming of Christ that can be awkward teaching for some of our communities. What makes them even more awkward is that, as far as we know, the very specific timing (very soon!) and the very specific imagery of the second coming that our Christian ancestors predicted in our sacred texts simply did not come to pass as they imagined it. This is an excellent time to remind our communities that those who wrote the New Testament and those who star in the New Testament were not busy trying to heroically create scripture with their lives and their scribes. Instead, they were simply struggling together to figure out what it meant to follow Jesus.

So what do we do with these awkward predictions in scripture? One angle might be to dwell on the sacred empathy that our ancestors express to us through these many generations. It is actually so helpful for me to remember that the first Christians did not know how things were going to work out because (and this is something I don't usually admit on my Facebook page) things don't always work out for *me* the way I think they should! And it is so healing for me to know that, in those disorienting moments, I am in some good and faithful company.

Another or additional angle for me is that it has never been the accurate predictions of the future that have drawn me to the Christian faith. It has always been, instead, about the *principles* of the faith—principles that my spiritual ancestors gave their lives for. "Don't be in debt to anyone, except for the obligation to love each other" (Rom 13:8). "You must love your neighbor as yourself" (v. 9). "Love doesn't do anything wrong to a neighbor…" (v. 10).

This week, instead of avoiding the uncomfortable idea that certain specific visions of the early Christian community simply did not come to pass, consider this an invitation to *lean in* to it, and see where the Spirit leads you in that journey.

Secondary Preaching Themes

This could be an interesting week to explore the theme of time in general. The Matthew passage is another poignant reminder that, even as the Gospel writers were trying to create coherent novellas of Jesus's life, they were also speaking to real communities—our spiritual ancestors, who were human just like us. If we imagine ourselves to be time travelers to first century Christianity, we would not encounter Renaissance paintings of saints. Instead, we would encounter groups of imperfect people who hurt one another, people who were trying to resolve conflict in healthy ways, people who needed to be held accountable. We would encounter people who are more like us than we think. What a treasure to have these early Christian documents that help us to feel that connection through time!

We can also play with the idea of time in reading the Exodus passage. Try to imagine with your community what it must have been like for the Israelites, who did not to know the ending of the story. It must have been terrifying. That is why the most powerful line from this reading might just be its last (Exod 12:14). God's final words of instruction are imagining a future day when Israelite descendants will commemorate this critical moment in the life of the people. In our own lives, in those moments of greatest fear and uncertainty, what a difference it can make to muster up the imagination of a future day when we will remember this moment as pivotal for our survival and flourishing. This time traveling imagination can be truly sacred!

Call to Worship

YOU know what time it is!
What time is it?
The hour has already come!
Which hour is that?
That hour when we wake up from our sleep!
Really? It's still dark out!
Our salvation is nearer than when we first had faith!
Look at that. A subtle glimmer of glory beginning to glow on the horizon.
Get dressed!
A brand new day! Hallelujah!

Dedication of the Offering

God, we thank you for this community that together remembers your acts of salvation, that recites together the fantastical stories of your revolutionary future. With these gifts, we pray that we might participate in and prepare for that future day of love, justice, and joy. Amen.

Benediction

Beloved, as our spiritual ancestors did in days before, go out today into this changing world, holding your claim to the principles and the persistent presence of our loving God.

September 13, 2020

Passages: Genesis 50:15-21; Psalm 103:1-7, 8-13; Romans 14:1-12;
Matthew 18:21-35

Laurie Zelman

Gathering Prayer

God of mercy, we come here thirsty for your word, to learn and relearn what really matters
in this world. Fill us with a desire to be your people and to worship you in truth. Amen.

Preaching Theme

In Jesus's parable of the Unforgiving Servant about the ways of compassion and
forgiveness, the amount the servant owes the king is a vast fortune, more than an
average person could make in many lifetimes. The servant was loaned this worldly
treasure, but it was only a loan. To repay even a small fraction of the loan's worth
would have meant ruin for the servant and the servant's family—a ripple effect of terrible debt. In an extraordinary act of compassion, the loan was forgiven by the king.
However, there was a price, and the price was to be transformed by being forgiven
and to spread the compassion. In other words, to bring the economy of heaven to
earth, to be open-handed and generous, to act as the king acted, to let mercy spread
like a wave.

Physics tells us that waves move energy from one place to another without moving matter. Waves can even move where there is no matter, that is, through a vacuum.
"This is done by a series of disturbances or vibrations that carry the energy," reads the
text in a YouTube illustration that even I, who never studied physics, can begin to
grasp. In the video, Fuse School[1] shows how a wave of energy is like people doing the
"wave" at a sports event. The wave moves through the stadium, and all each person
has to do is stand up.

In God's economy, forgiveness begets more forgiveness, compassion changes us
and charges us with being compassionate. When we who are forgiven do not respond
by being the ripples, being conductors of that mercy, we prevent God's will from
spreading. This is the cost of God's mercy. Jesus's parable teaches us that we must
stand up. We don't have to move, going to a far-off place to enact God's will. But we
are called to stand up.

Secondary Preaching Themes

The Genesis passage is another story of forgiveness, the climax of the long, thrilling narrative of Joseph, which contains many twists and reversals. The story of brothers selling a brother into slavery resonates with a difficult and fraught history in the United States. Joseph's brothers are afraid that Joseph will ask them to pay reparations (50:15). Joseph's brothers ask his forgiveness for the grievous harm of selling him to slave traders and lying to their father for years about it. Unlike the servant in the Gospel passage, the change and repentance in these brothers is real. This transformation brings not only reconciliation within a family, but also ushers in, for a time, an era of peace, when many lives were saved (50:20).

In the Gospel parable, the failure of the servant to forgive as he is forgiven is immediate, and the withdrawal of God's mercy falls quickly. In contrast, the Genesis passage caps a generational saga and illustrates the slow growing of wisdom in Joseph and his brothers. Wisdom grows slowly over a lifetime, and forgiveness and reconciliation are the crowning result.

Call to Worship

God is merciful.
Let my whole being bless our God.
God is faithful.
Let my whole being bless our God.
God's work is righteousness.
God's will be done
Let us give God honor and praise.

Prayer of Confession and Word of Assurance (Based on Psalm 103:8-13)

We say "forgive our trespasses"
But we hold on to grievances.
We say "thy will be done"
But we fail to let God move us.
Forgive us, God of Mercy,
Soften our hearts, free us to respond
In the generosity of your spirit.
Amen.

Hear the good news: God is merciful and full of compassion. God has patience. God will guide us as a loving parent teaches a beloved child. In the name of Jesus, we are forgiven.

September 20, 2020

Passages: Exodus 16:2-15 or Psalm 105:1-6, 37-45; Jonah 3:10–4:11 or Psalm 145:1-8; Philippians 1:21-30; Matthew 20:1-16

Grant Hagiya

Gathering Prayer

God of grace and God of glory, fill our anxious lives with the knowledge of your encompassing and ever compassionate love. As we react in anger to the injustices of our world, help us to remember the depth of your divine grace, so that we may reflect it in word and deed today and always. Amen.

Preaching Theme

Grace or justice? As we look at our Christian faith, shouldn't this be grace and justice? In much of the Bible, both of these twin themes are fixed as attributes of God. God is the very embodiment of both grace and justice. It is hard to find a situation in which one is more important than the other.

And yet, Jesus does that very thing in the Matthew 20:1-16 text for today. It is the story of workers being hired to tend to the owner's vineyard. In a legal contract, the vineyard owner agrees to pay them a set amount as they start the day at 6 a.m. Additional workers are hired every three hours to work with the same contracted amount. Finally, right before sundown and the close of the day, additional workers are hired at 5 p.m. and work for a very short amount of time.

When it comes time to pay the workers, everyone is given the exact same amount, no more or no less. The workers who started at six in the morning have toiled in the vineyard for more than twelve hours, and they receive the exact same amount as those who start at five at night and work for about one hour.

As a question of justice, should the workers who put in only one hour's worth of work receive the same amount as those who have labored for twelve hours? Obviously not, especially if you were one of the workers who showed up early in the morning. Isn't it natural for them to complain about this seeming injustice?

In our human framework, of course it is. And yet, the owner fulfills his legal obligation by giving all the workers the upfront agreed-upon amount of wages. There is no violation of the law here. It is not a question of the justice of the owner but a reflection of his or her generosity.

Such is the nature of grace, or the absolute love of God. Even the perceived standards of human justice cannot stand up to the overwhelming love of God. God's grace is that absolute and sure, and everything pales in comparison.

Secondary Preaching Themes

In Jonah, we see a direct example of this same all-consuming grace. We remember that the Ninevites are the sworn enemies of Jonah and the Israelites, and the enmity is so great that they cannot be forgiven. This is the reason that Jonah is so relentlessly angry. He is the one that has to bring God's message that saves them. And because they repent, God saves them rather than destroying them as Jonah had hoped. Jonah's anger is even greater than life, for he wishes to die rather than see the Ninevites saved.

However, God's grace trumps all of human self-righteousness and even justice. God as creator, just as the vineyard owner in the Gospel, has the right of generosity. Jonah's injustice cannot stand in the way of God saving 120,000 people and also many animals (all of the creative order). Because all life is precious to God, the many animals are as important as the 120,000 people.

Likewise, the psalmist in Psalm 145 sings praises to God over the works and deeds of God. The very source of such works and deeds is in God's compassionate and faithful love.

Unison Prayer of Repentance

All loving God, we come before you and ask for forgiveness over our self-righteous anger when we experience injustice from our selfish point of view. In our human frailty, we cannot accept your divine forgiveness of those we judge to be unjust. Forgive us for our lack of faith and self-conscious point of view. Create in us a clean heart, O Lord. We confess these things with confidence in your assurance to forgive and in light of your divine love. Amen.

Sending Forth

We have witnessed your all-embracing grace today.
Praise be to the God of love!
Release this grace in all of us.
May we reflect this grace in all we say and do.
Go now and live this love of God.
Amen.

September 27, 2020

Passages: Exodus 17:1-7; Psalm 78; Psalm 25; Philippians 2:1-13; Matthew 21:23-32

Tanya Linn Bennett

Gathering Prayer

Water is sixty percent of our human bodies and seventy percent of the earth's surface. It is the most vital source of life. We are so thirsty. Parched. Where do we find each other, and you, God, in the living drink of life? May we touch and drink deeply of the water again, reminding, remembering, re-membering you, ourselves, and the church of Christ. Come to us again, Great Source of Living Water.

Preaching Theme

The metaphor of water as the source of life is persistent throughout the biblical narrative, and this passage from Exodus is a central reminder of God's renewal of sources of living water. As the Israelites wrestle with their newfound freedom, complaining every step of the way as they move toward liberation, we find them pleading with Moses (again). "Why did you bring us out of Egypt just to kill us and our livestock with thirst?" Making no attempt themselves to seek out water, they hunker down in camp and wait for Moses to make the impossible possible. And, again, Moses counsels with God, and God offers him the solution: Take the elders and go to Horeb. I will meet you there, and when you strike the rock with your shepherd's staff, water will pour out. And all will drink.

In these parched and thirsty days in our churches, where do we find the water of life? With so many of our people both around the globe and just next door thirsting physically and spiritually, how does the body of Christ respond? What does it mean when too many of our human kin do not have access to this most critical sustainer of human life? How do we make water an economic asset? How do we demonstrate our disregard for certain of God's children by allowing pollutants to run into our sources of drinking water in cities like Newark, New Jersey, and Flint, Michigan?

When God offers to meet us halfway to pierce open the rocks of our hearts, if we will just throw down our spears, will we go running to the modern-day Horebs to let the water flow? When those of us who have been nurtured in the living water and drunk deeply of running water, what are we called to do and be to those who are parched?

Secondary Preaching Theme

In Matthew's passage we find the disciples distressed and arguing among themselves, "If we say 'from heaven,' he'll say to us, 'Then why didn't you believe him?' But we can't say 'from humans' because we're afraid of the crowd, since everyone thinks John was a prophet." Then they replied, "We don't know" (Matt 21:25-27).

Even as those disciples stress about who has the authority to baptize, we argue now about who has the authority to decide who may be fully part of the United Methodist arm of the body of Christ. As members of a church with both a conflicted heritage of exclusion and a Wesleyan theology embracing expansive notions of grace, we are called to set aside our own opinions, to strengthen the love and compassion of the church in ways that move us forward as the living body of Christ.

Litany for Gathering

We are not here because we have found God but because God has found us and called us into this time and place.
Challenging us to accept the cost and joy of discipleship, and to be in service to all of creation.
But God's call is also God's promise.
A promise of forgiveness and grace, courage in the struggle for justice and peace, and eternal life in a realm that has no end.
Blessing and honor and glory to God!

Ritual of Remembering

Brothers and sisters in Christ,
through the sacred act of baptism,
we begin the journey of discipleship.
We become part of God's holy work,
and we are born again through the water of life
and the Spirit of peace and hope.
This is God's gift to us, a gift that comes without cost.

We remember our baptism, and we are thankful.

Today, as we remember the story of the baptism of Jesus,
We renew the vow taken at our baptism to be faithful disciples of Jesus Christ.
Do you embrace the promise God makes to us to always be faithful and merciful,

To show grace beyond measure and forgiveness that never ends?
We do.
Do you accept the freedom and power God gives you to seek justice in all times and places, for all people and all creation?
We do.
Do you promise to be faithful and merciful, to love God and Jesus Christ with all your heart and mind and soul, and to love your neighbor?
We do.
Do you, as the body of Christ, renew your promise to always be faithful to God and to each other?
We do.

As you are called, as you are moved, you may approach the waters of baptism. Remember always that, just as God called out to Jesus, God calls out to us, "You are my beloved, with you I am well pleased."

Suggested Hymn

"Rain Down," Lyrics and arrangement by Jamie Cortez. *UpperRoom Worship Book.*

October 4, 2020

Passages: Exodus 20:1-4, 7-9, 12-20 or Psalm 19; Isaiah 5:1-7 or Psalm 80:7-15; Philippians 3:4b-14; Matthew 21:33-46

Lydia Muñoz

Opening Prayer (Based on Psalm 19)

Let the words of my mouth
    and the meditations of my heart
    be pleasing to you,
    Lord, my rock and my redeemer.

Preaching Theme

If you have gardeners and farmers in your congregation, this is the time to tap into them for illustrations and perhaps even props for cementing the themes of planting and tending a field in the Matthew passage. Everyone likely knows what it feels like to have spent energy, time, and resources preparing something, whether in our kitchens, our high-tech work stations, or in a literal field. Working the ground, watering, seeding and all the various things in order to produce a crop require energy. It is labor, and you really do have to love the work of farming or else you would never do it. What happens when others don't value your work, or when what you do is pushed aside and considered rubbish?

A word of warning here: It is easy to slip into an anti-Semitic posture with this particular parable. If we read carefully, Jesus leaves the retribution open—in fact, he leaves it in our hands. "When the owner of the vineyard comes, what will he do to those tenant farmers?" (21:40). They were the ones who responded with the violent retribution of the landowner. Perhaps the nature of the kingdom of God is not in the retribution, but rather in the insistence and persistence. God's kingdom will never give up; it will always break through, even when it appears to be rejected. We have no control over the merciful actions of God and God's reach toward us, even though we through our words and deeds toward others have thrown our fair share of persons "out of the vineyard."

Secondary Preaching Theme

Rejection isn't easy. Everyone remembers the first time they were rejected at school, by the kickball team, or by the boy or girl who wouldn't be our friend. As we get older, rejection can become a serious problem. We have seen or heard account after account of violence and even murder by men who feel rejected by women who do not respond to their advances in the way they would like. However, rejection is inevitable. You will be rejected, one way or another. How we prepare resilience in our children to deal with a rejection is an important character-building lesson that we need to teach them.

In Philippians, Paul talks to us about rejection that occurs when we choose to follow the Jesus way. If anyone had a résumé and pedigree that would endear him with the most noble of people, the most popular, the most wanted, it certainly was Paul. But if one is serious about following the way of Jesus, we can expect that not everyone will be so accepting of us. When we begin to align our values with those of Christ, rejection just might be inevitable. But for Paul, the goal was not to be accepted by others but to experience the power of resurrection, the power of a life lived in harmony with God. What happens when we shift our goals toward that goal? Does our concept of rejection and acceptance change? Do we discover the power of being true to ourselves and to everything that God calls us to be, even though there is a very real possibility that we might experience the rejection of others? This just might be the finest life work of a disciple: to thine own self be true.

Responsive Prayer
(A Contemplative Reading of Isaiah 5:1-7)

The ground is dry, stony, and lifeless,
yet you come.
You have dug deep into the soil, uncovering treasure that has long been buried, surprising me,
I see things I've forgotten were there,
things I wanted to forget.
The seed so carefully planted in me has so often not produced good fruit
Because I've so often resisted your nurturing Spirit,
weeding and pruning, mulching and fertilizing.
Yet, you come.
It's all ruin now; there is nothing but thorns and thistle and I am desperately dry.
Yet . . . you come.
You come, because this doesn't depend on my ability to produce good fruit but
on my availability to surrender to the process.
You come, because grace is never measured, and the more I think this is the end,
that's when it rushes in to show me once again
that dead things can come back to life,
and every ground is worth tilling.

Suggested Hymn

"Take, O Take Me As I Am" Lyrics by John Bell

Benediction (Based on Philippians 3)

(When possible, have musician play the melody of the Civil Rights Freedom Song while the benediction is offered.)

Keep your eyes on the prize
keep your eyes on the prize
Keep your eyes on the prize,
hold on

Beloved, we may not be there yet
But we keep our eyes on the prize
Beloved, we may not have all reached all our goals
But we hold fast to what we have achieved

Keep your eyes on the prize
keep your eyes on the prize
Keep your eyes on the prize,
hold on

So now go, forgetting what is behind and pressing on to what is ahead
Go in the power of the Holy One who has called you by name
and has fixed your eyes on the prize
of your heavenly call

Hold on, hold on
keep your eyes on the prize
hold on.

October 11, 2020

Passages: Exodus 32:1-14 or Isaiah 25:1-9; Psalm 106:1-6, 19-23 or
Psalm 23; Philippians 4:1-9; Matthew 22:1-14

James McIntire

Gathering Prayer

God, open us to the questions from within, wrestle with us in the wonder of your word,
lead us in our attempts to deepen our relationship with you and each other. Amen.

Preaching Theme

If you regularly use the Benedictine practice of Lectio Divina to read, meditate, pray, contemplate, you know that the Matthew text for this week is one of those places where this might help. If you've never used it, this may be the time to start. Matthew's Wedding Feast is a difficult parable with no easy preaching points. However, one of the strengths of lectionary preaching is that it challenges us with texts that we would just as soon avoid. Don't avoid this one, but rather read, meditate, pray, contemplate, repeat. Let God and the parable bring out the questions and let your wrestling with the questions be your sermon.

"The kin-dom of heaven is like. . . ." Is it like the king or like the party preparation or like the party itself? Is it like the guests? Or is the kin-dom like the brutal and capricious actions of the king portrayed in the story?

Who were the invited guests who "didn't want to come" (22:3) and why didn't they want to? Maybe they knew the king's reputation; maybe they weren't fond of the bride and groom. Were these A-list guests, the kids at the "cool table" in the cafeteria who didn't want to be seen with the nerdy royalists? I suspect they had no reason to believe they would die and have their city destroyed (v. 7) by not attending—even the most cynical of cool kids among us would attend the nerdy party to avoid destruction.

So much for the A-list. Now what? The food is ready, the meats are on the grill, the champagne is chilled. The king sends his servants "to the roads on the edge of town" to find new guests—the B-list. What is the significance of "roads on the edge of town"? (v. 9) Is it where the undesirable live? Where is the edge in your world, your community, your life? Would you ever think of going there to invite people to God's party?

In Greek, *diexodos* is "the way out of somewhere else," the place where city streets turn into country roads. "Those people" are the ones who live out there because they don't want to be part of the in-crowd. So why would the king want them? Was he just desperate to have anyone? Or does that make God seem pretty capricious?

Or maybe the king in the parable isn't God after all; maybe we are the king and God is the rejected. Maybe it's God out there living on the edges of our lives where we wouldn't even imagine looking. Is that the sermon? When we feel rejected by God like the king feels rejected by the A-list, do we, like the king, look elsewhere for an accepting and acceptable god? Are we saying "God, we want you at our party but only by our rules"? And when God says "No thanks, not on your terms," we toss God aside and invite to our party whoever or whatever else meets our standards.

Don't forget the guest who forgot about the dress code (v. 11). That guest got the invitation, was willing to come, was ready for the food and bubbly and music and dancing, but not *really* ready. Not ready by our rules anyway. Even when God does show up, we say, "Nope, that's not the god I wanted," and we bind God "hands and feet" and throw that one "out into the farthest darkness" (v. 13).

Frederick Buechner once said, "With parables and jokes both, if you've got to have them explained, don't bother."[1] In preaching this uncomfortable text, ask and wrestle with the questions, but don't explain it away.

Secondary Preaching Themes

The Hebrew texts this week support the temptation of only accepting a god created in our image. Exodus is the classic example of our rejection of God and attempted replacement by a lesser god: "When the people saw that Moses delayed to come down from the mountain, the people gathered around Aaron, and said to him, 'Come, make gods for us, who shall go before us'" (32:1a NRSV).

The psalmist reminds us of that familiar theme and prays that we might never do it again: "Our ancestors, when they were in Egypt, did not consider your wonderful works.... They exchanged the glory of God for the image of an ox that eats grass" (106:7, 20 NRSV).

Call to Worship

Out of bondage you led us, O God,
You heard our pleas.
Into faithfulness you summoned us, O God,
To you, our God, we reserve our devotion.
Call us now out of our bondage to the world's allure,
Your call is in our ears and on our hearts.
We respond in faith, O God,
And may we never forget that only you are God.
Let us worship God.

October 18, 2020

Passages: Exodus 33:12-23; Psalm 99; 1 Thessalonians 1:1-10;
Matthew 22:15-22

Jennifer and Todd Pick

Gathering Prayer

Maker of All, the earth and sky and sea are yours. You show us your glorious presence in
each sunset, each mountain, each person we meet. Uniquely made in your image, you call
us by name and claim us as your own. We are truly yours. May we reflect more of your
likeness so that the world might be transformed into your realm of justice for all and love
without end. Amen.

Preaching Theme

These are taxing times for most of us: those who live with the constant threat
of racism or poverty; those displaced without country or homeland; those who live
paycheck to paycheck; those who can only get through a day by compartmentalizing
their lives so that the enormity of the world's pain doesn't swallow them whole. We
cannot exorcise all that is evil from daily life, and sadly, we all participate in unjust
systems. If we are fortunate enough to have money, we carry around the image of
Caesar on a daily basis. So, what do we do with this Gospel text that asks us to recognize what is Caesar's and what is God's? Exactly what should we give back to Caesar
and what should we give back to God?

When looking at Matthew 22, we must remember a couple of things. Jerusalem
was occupied by the Roman Empire: the Jewish people were a conquered people,
and the ways of Rome stood in stark difference to ways of Israel. Money issued by
Rome in the form of currency had "Tiberius Caesar, son of the divine Augustus, high
priest" stamped right on it. That presented a problem for God's people since the To-
rah clearly stated that they should not put any other gods before God.

"Give to Caesar what belongs to Caesar and to God what belongs to God," Jesus
instructed (v. 21). It is difficult to imagine that Jesus would see much of anything falling outside of "what belongs to God." If that which bears the image of Caesar belongs
to Caesar, then certainly that which bears the image of God belongs to God. We are
the image of God—every part of us. In effect, Jesus is saying give your whole self to
the One who has imprinted divinity upon you.

If God owns all, then we belong to God alone. Yet we live in a world in which competing powers and influences vie to own us, to sway us and capture our hearts. This text is the call of Jesus to live in faithfulness while navigating in contexts that often tug at that faithfulness. Such navigation is not easy, and we would do well to seek God's wisdom and discernment as we desire to follow Christ in a world full of siren songs. No part of our life is excluded from our fundamental covenant with the One who is our Creator, in whose image we are made. We are the coin that bears God's image.

Secondary Preaching Themes

By Exodus 33, Moses has had enough. A serendipitous meeting at a burning bush where God refused to give Moses an intelligible name by which to know God has led to this moment where Moses begs to see God's face—God's image. Moses is tired of being left in the dark. Like the Gospel text from this week, Moses knows that images hold power. He wants to get to know the One who is leading him and his people to freedom by seeing God's glorious face. Indeed, it is in that exact image that humanity was made.

The psalmist cries the holiness of God. We can imagine, reading this Psalm, the reason why God shielded God's face from Moses in Exodus 33.

Call to Worship

Lift up your songs to the Song of Joy.
We give to God what belongs to God.
Surrender your hearts to the Heart of Love.
We give to God what belongs to God.
Return your lives to the Author of Life.
We give to God what belongs to God.
Come, let us worship the Holy One who makes us holy.
All that we have and all that we are comes from the Lord of All.
Come, let us worship and give to God what belongs to God.

Unison Prayer

Creator of light and darkness, shaper of stars and seas, you made the heavens and the earth in beauty and blessing. In you, love abounds and mercy overflows. Instead of believing in your abundance, the world would have us believe in emptiness and scarcity, in never having enough and always needing more. We find ourselves patterned by fear and greed instead of by grace. We value our own security over compassionate service. We accumulate treasures rather than sharing in community. Forgive us, O God, and remake us in your image. Recreate the world into your realm where justice and peace are plentiful, compassion is shared generously, and love is unconditional. Amen.

Benediction

We go imprinted by God's love.
We go imitating Christ.
We go invigorated by the Spirit.
We go imagining the world made new.
Renewed in God's image, we go!

October 25, 2020

Passages: Deuteronomy 34:1-12 or Psalm 90:1-6, 13-17; Leviticus 19:1-2 or Psalm 1; 1 Thessalonians 2:1-8; Matthew 22:34-46

Vicki Flippin

Gathering Prayer

God, like a young tree, we struggle and strive each day to grow taller, to expand our stature, to widen our shadow. But you are our ground. You look on us with knowing grace, luring us with your love and mystery. Your lure and allure are not up toward the heavens but are instead down further into your grounding. You desire for us to stretch our roots deeper and wider into the complex network of your teeming life, lest we topple over with our own individual ambition. In these moments, connect us deeper in to your rich dark being. Amen.

Preaching Theme

Playing with the imagery in Psalm 1, what does it mean for us to strive to be rooted like trees instead of "dust that the wind blows away"?

There is a great TED Talk by Canadian forest ecologist Suzanne Simard called "How Trees Talk to Each Other."[2] In it, she reveals the incredible ecological science that helps us to see that forests are much more than a collection of plant life in Darwinian competition for resources. Instead, a forest ecosystem is almost like one single organism, with various parts working together, communicating and participating in the health of the whole.

It is a beautiful frame shift, is it not? Instead of a world in which individual organisms compete for survival, maybe we are all in this together. Maybe we are all on the same team, connected, in relationship, one big life, competing not for *my* own glory, *my* own success, *my* own legacy. Instead, we are participating in the beauty and the struggle of the whole organism of life itself!

For me, the idea of being rooted and grounded in something larger than myself has always been a great way of describing my most enduring individual faith experiences. Our churches, too, might think of themselves as rooted and grounded in a larger ecosystem of God's life. Instead of assuming your single church needs to bring all the salvation to your town, how can you think of yourselves as just one participant in a larger network of God's work and mission in the world?

Secondary Preaching Themes

Much of our daily striving in life is about gaining earthly reward. We work for the promotion, the raise, the accolades, the prestige and self-satisfaction. We want to see and feel and taste the results. And that is totally reasonable. But we as the church are hopefully inviting people into a deeper life of reflection and transcendent meaning. So it may be interesting to ask ourselves, "What am I participating in that will outlive me? Am I investing in something sacred over which I have no control?"

In today's passage from Exodus, we realize that Moses has worked for most of his life toward a promised land that he will never reach himself. He has done his best to guide his people for a season, but even Moses has no control over what happens next. Even Moses is just one character in a few books of a very thick canon. But it is his humble participation in that larger life, that eternal and divine story, that is his greatest legacy.

So how do *we* participate in something greater than ourselves? Well, many secular folks in the world can make sense of that second greatest commandment named by Jesus in Matthew: "You must love your neighbor as you love yourself." But our unique role as a spiritual community is to explore with people the first: "You must love the Lord your God with all your heart, with all your being, and with all your mind." What does it mean for you to love (invest in, communicate with, and participate in) the life of the eternal divine? Why is this important to you? Answering these questions are key to today's ministry contexts in many parts of the world, as more and more folks are less and less committed to this "religion" thing.

Call to Worship

When the storms of life threaten to knock us down,
Just like a tree that's planted by the water,
We shall not be moved!
When depressions and injustices try to displace our calm,
Just like a tree that's planted by the water,
We shall not be moved!
When despair and disease desire to strip our resolve,
Just like a tree that's planted by the water,
We shall not be moved!
We are rooted and grounded in your nourishing soil, O God.
We shall not!
We shall not be moved!

Sending Forth

We have all felt, from time to time, like dust blown away by the wind.
But go out today to deepen your roots.
Replant yourself where you can be nourished
to bear fruit and grow healthy leaves.
And may you be grounded in the grace, glory, and justice of our God
Who invites us each day into the abundant life of the divine.

– 123

November 1, 2020– All Saints' Day

Passages: Revelation 7:9-17; Psalm 34:1-10, 22; 1 John 3:1-3; Matthew 5:1-12

J. Terry Todd

Gathering Prayer

Creator God, on this All Saints' Sunday, deepen our understanding of the bonds of faith that transcend time. Bind us together in the mystical company of the communion of saints, those in every age who speak your name and who walk your paths of holiness. Grant us grace to follow in the footsteps of those who have come before us, witnessing to your transformative love, so that we may be counted as everyday saints in your eternal reign. Amen.

Preaching Theme

The sidewalk and roadside memorials found so commonly across our shared landscapes remind us that with or without the church's involvement, people will discover ways to remember the dead. Informal altars with candles, stuffed animals, personal effects, and handwritten messages bear witness to the seemingly universal need for liturgies and ritual objects that recognize and celebrate the ties that bind the living and the dead.

In a highly mobile society where it is not always possible to visit family graves, the celebration of All Saints' Day offers resources to fulfill human longings for remembrance and abiding connection. Traditionally recognized as one of the church's principal festivals, the observance of All Saints' Day dates back to about the seventh century. The Latin Western church's calendar had become so crowded with days to remember prophets, apostles, and martyrs that November 1 became a general feast day recognizing all the saints. Still later, November 2 became All Souls' Day, a more somber day of prayers for all the faithful departed, not just the church's canonized saints. Latin Christian practices associated with these days blended with indigenous traditions to become elaborate cultural observances in many parts of the world. In Central America and now among many Latinx people in the United States,

El Día de los Muertos, the Day of the Dead, celebrates the continuing relations between the living and those who've passed into glory.

At the time of the Reformation, many Protestants abandoned the church calendar as an unbiblical invention, and for centuries looked with suspicion at the liturgical practices of All Saints' Day and All Souls' Day. Yet it's notable that in recent years more and more churches have begun to mark the Sunday after November 1 as All Saints' Sunday, a conflation of the two older observances.

The communion of saints is the mystical idea that God's people are knit together in a web of relationality that crosses the boundaries of life and death, time and eternity. We, the living, do not pray to the saints on the other side of the vale, but rather we pray with the saints. In a very real sense, we are present to and with each other, participating together in God's holiness as it flows through time and space. As a theological idea, the communion of saints developed across the first few centuries of the church's life, and so there are no biblical texts that directly mention it. The idea is familiar to most of us from our recitation of a key phrase in the Apostles' Creed, but otherwise the idea is rarely considered among Protestants. Yet the lectionary texts for All Saints' Sunday provide opportunities to reflect on the communion of saints and even to enact it in the day's liturgy.

The sense of mystery at the heart of the communion of saints is conveyed in the Epistle reading, and especially in the fantastical passage from the book of Revelation. "Dear friends, now we are God's children," we're told in 1 John 3, "and it hasn't yet appeared what we will be." Whatever shape our future takes, it's not just about me but about us—it's about Christian community. Cut to the strange vision recounted in the Revelation 7:9-17. These verses are often read in the funeral rite, but do they offer a vision deferred only until after death? The idea of the communion of saints pushes us toward an emphatic no. The communal dimension of Christian hope is available not just in heaven, but also in *this* life through our participation in the mystery of the communion of saints.

The challenge of preaching the Revelation text is to bring it down to earth, so to speak, to connect it to our lives despite the image of white-robed saints waving palm fronds and bowing before the Lamb, John of Patmos's rejoinder to Roman imperial pretensions. Yet despite the first-century fashions, the passage still pulses with meaning for us today. It provides a soaring articulation of hope for "a great crowd…from every nation, tribe, people and language…who have come out of great hardship" (vv. 9, 14). John's vision gives us a sense of the global diversity of the communion of saints, the living and the dead, a definitive rejection of the tribalism and ethno-nationalism that plagues so much of the world today. The communion of saints includes those we know and love and who look and speak like us, just as it also includes those very much unlike us in language, racial identification, and national origin.

Secondary Preaching Theme

Blessed be me, or happy are we?

What does it mean to walk in the way of Christ and the saints? The Gospel reading leads us to Matthew's version of the Beatitudes, the opening of Jesus's Sermon on the Mount. The CEB's rendering of the Greek term *makarios* as "happy" instead of the traditional "blessed" invites the reader to hear this familiar teaching in a new way, and so does its inclusion in a celebration of All Saints' Sunday. Modern interpretations of the Beatitudes often get us thinking about how *I'm* doing on the piety index. But when we pivot again from the individual to the community, the Beatitudes can take on a different meaning. The word *beatitude* carries a sense of fulfillment, of enlargement as well as being blessed and happy. At our most vulnerable, as we walk through grief and hopelessness and even persecution, as we walk humbly, as we make peace, we are fulfilled and enlarged. We also know that we don't walk alone, but instead with those who in every place and time witness with their lives to these Christian virtues, reflections of God's holiness.

Experiential Worship Element

One of the most striking ways to enact the mystery of the communion of saints through liturgy is at the Eucharist. Even those communities that celebrate Holy Communion once a month can participate, since All Saints' Sunday falls on the first Sunday after November 1. Invite everyone to bring photographs of the faithfully departed or mementos associated with loved ones who walked in the way of Jesus. A candlelit table is set to hold the objects, photos, or cards with names and messages of gratitude. If the congregation is small, gather people close around the Lord's Table. Use silence generously, and at some point in the communion liturgy, offer this invitation prayer:

Holy One, you knit us together, the living and the dead, in the mystical bond of the communion of saints. We remember all those who have called upon your name in heaven and on earth, and especially those whose lives are so closely linked with ours.

Read the names of those community members who have died in the past year, and then ask the congregation to offer additional names.

Benediction

We give you thanks for our continuing journey with these everyday saints. Grant us the grace we need to continue our walk with you. Remind us when we falter that we do not walk alone, but with you, O Lord, and the glorious company of the saints in light.

November 8, 2020

Passages: Joshua 24:1-3a, 14–25; Psalm 78:1-7; 1 Thessalonians 4:13-18; Matthew 25:1-13

Tanya Linn Bennett

Focusing Prayer

Prepare us, creator God, for whatever surprise arrival you may have in store. Let us never be without all that we need to receive you again.

Preaching Theme

The story of the ten young bridesmaids has always been a difficult one for me to embrace for a variety of reasons—all the more cause to preach about it! First, for the writer of Matthew to make ten young women the primary characters in this parable about lack of preparation and attention, ten young women already among the least in that time and maybe in our time still, ten young women...so that's the first problematic with this text. But, ten young women it is. So they take their lamps and go to meet the "groom." Do we assume that the groom is a metaphor for Jesus, the lover of our souls? Many commentaries would suggest so. And yet, the women fall asleep waiting for the auspicious arrival of the expected one. Deep in the night, a cry rings out, the groom has arrived. But, the "foolish" bridesmaids have run out of oil for their lamps. So, they beg the wise ones, "Please give us some of yours. But the five wise ones decline to help their sisters, sending them on an errand to buy their own. While they are gone, the groom arrives and, upon their knock at the door, refuses to let them in. In fact, refuses to recognize them.

The word *bridesmaids* is frequently replaced with "virgins" in this passage. The word *virgin* not only suggests inexperience, naivete and vulnerability, but also might lead us to believe that an act of initiation is to take place between these virgins and the groom to come, an intimacy that the five without oil will miss out on. This parable is difficult, but not unlike others of Matthew's parables which seem bent towards sorting the righteous from the unworthy, a judgmental stance which makes us uncomfortable. Is this the Gospel message we want to preach? Could we instead approach this text, running headlong towards its problematic components, but also wondering if we can call each other to be ready to receive a gift that is to come? Or could this text call us to expansive generosity that calls us to share with those around us so that none of us miss out? (The "wise" virgins don't come off very well here, either.) Were we to take turns keeping the watch and shouting out when we see the Great Love approaching, wouldn't we all meet that One together?

Secondary Preaching Theme

In this letter to the Thessalonians, Paul is far more generous than Matthew's gospel. In fact, if this pericope were to start at verse 9 rather than 13, we would hear Paul congratulating the Thessalonians for supporting each other: "You don't need us to write about loving your brothers and sisters because God has already taught you to love each other," Paul says, "in fact, you are doing loving deeds for all the brothers and sisters throughout Macedonia. Now we encourage you, brothers and sisters, to do so even more." Paul goes on to suggest that even those who are "dead" in Christ, having fallen asleep in faith, might also rise up, so that along with the "living," all would see the glory of God "in the air" together, no one excluded or left out. May we, as Paul recommends, encourage each other with these words.

Suggested Hymn

The African American spiritual "Keep Your Lamps Trimmed and Burning" is based on the parable of the bridesmaids, and is a good reminder as we come into the season of Advent, as days grow short and dim, that our light shines on, guiding the One to come while we wait. (*New Century Hymnal*, 369)

Benediction

Let us not grow weary while we wait, or let our oil run low. But encourage each other to keep on, waiting and living in Holy Grace, a presence of God's love for all around us.

November 15, 2020

Passages: Judges 4:1-7; Psalm 90:1-8, (9-11), 12; 1 Thessalonians 5:1-11;
Matthew 25:14-30

Heather Murray Elkins

Gathering Prayer

Holy One, Holy Three
you have been our help,
from our beginning and beyond our end.
From age to age you are the same.
Before mountains were formed,
you are.
Before seas divided and seasons began,
you are.
Before the birthing of the earth
or the explosion of stars,
you are.
Holy One, Holy Three
As Love was in the beginning, is now, and ever shall be,
World without end. Amen.

Preaching Theme

The stories that Jesus told were not easy to hear. They shouldn't be easy to preach. Parables are not allegories, although this was the way they were preached for centuries. They are not "illustrations," although this parable has been employed as the bane and blessing of everything from descriptions of hell, banking practices, and educational assessments of "talent." The preaching task will be to break through generations of "already heard that." This parable has hardened like concrete into a platitude, so the sermon will need to work like a pickaxe to uncover some of its life.

One approach would be to disrupt and disturb with questions about the character of the man/owner/master. Is he corrupt? Does the owner harvest grain where he hasn't sown and gather crops where he hasn't spread seed? Is the servant projecting his own resentments and the owner simply mocking him before tossing him out? Is God a thief as well as a hard taskmaster? "But as for those who don't have much, even the little bit they have will be taken away from them" (25:29). Is this character supposed to be God? How does this match assumptions of a generous compassionate deity? Then what do we do with the surprising twist where those who served are gifted with the "talents" they invested? This kind of generosity would have caught his listeners off-guard. This was and is an extravagant economy of grace.

Jesus told stories that were designed to upset the status quo of the empire and the religious structures and authorities of his time. They were and are the heart of Jesus's teaching and preaching and the Gospels. In Matthew's Gospel, this parable forms a narrative that dislodges our sense of balance, our assumptions about matters such as church endowments to who owns the life we are living. Mary Oliver's theo-poetic question extends the parable into the hearing of a contemporary community of faith: "Tell me, what is it you plan to do with your one wild and precious life?"[1]

Secondary Preaching Themes

The parable of the Talents could also be read as text on time. If American pollsters are right, there is one reality that consistently elicits feelings of anxiety and guilt: Time. There's too much or not enough or some combination of both. We invest it, waste it, save it, kill it, and always think we're running out. Our language and feelings about time often reveal what we believe about God. Our technologies of telling time shape our theologies. There's a deadline looming; we will be audited, evaluated, judged on what we've done with our far-too-brief life.

Matthew's Gospel is filled with narratives of judgment. There are vivid descriptions of wailing and "gnashing of teeth" for those who have not risked all that they have for Christ and the gospel. For Matthew's community, end times are to be prayed for and celebrated—not feared. The will of God will be done. The kingdom (or kindom) of heaven will come. It is here that the Gospel passage and Psalm 90 can be connected with narratives of human uncertainty and God's eternal time.

The psalmist evokes the sense of human mortality as we see how brief and fragile our lives can be and ends with a heartfelt prayer: "Teach us to number our days so we can have a wise heart" (90:12). The parable of the talents reminds us that we will lose our lives if we do not give them, if we bury them, if we forget who is the giver of all life. Both the Gospel and this ancient song of faith rest on the reality of the One who was, and is, and will be forever.

Prayer of Confession

God of grace and glory,
forgive our gritty sins.
We have buried the best of ourselves
in the backyards of our lives.
Lord, have mercy.

We are afraid to invest ourselves deeply.
We avoid the risk of being good
if it doesn't pay or guarantee success.
Christ, have mercy.

Set our hidden faults in the light from your face.
Sweep away our fear like a dream,
Renew us in the morning.
Lord, have mercy.

Words of Assurance

The Holy One declares, "Come to me and you will live. I will be with you forever."

Blessing

May the One who created the universe call you by name.
May Christ bless you with joy.
May the Holy Spirit invest you with the power of love, now and forever.

November 22, 2020–
Christ the King Sunday

Passages: Ezekiel 34:11-16, 20-24 or Psalm 100; Psalm 95:1-7a;
Ephesians 1:15-23; Matthew 25:31-46

Gary Simpson

Gathering Prayer

Awesome and Great God, how blessed we are to witness your greatness in all the earth. Your vastness causes us to wander and wonder throughout your creation. Wherever we find ourselves, your beauty there surrounds us. Moreover, we marvel that in all your greatness, you are yet tender and gracious in your provision for our sustenance. With grateful hearts we bless your name and give you thanks. Amen.

Preaching Theme

How desperately in our times do we need images of authority that are not mere exercises of power over and against. On Christ the King Sunday, we have an opportunity to hold up a vision of Christ that also stands as counter to the ways in which our human seats of authority—both in governments and within ourselves (do you sit on the throne of your own life?). The essence of Christ's place in the world and in our hearts is beyond explanation. Words alone fail. We need a song.

One cannot read Psalm 95 without standing in awe at the presence and greatness of God. The psalmist praises the Almighty God and yet reminds us of the tenderness that the Almighty provides for us.

The most wonderful and yet frightening words in any church worship are "Let us sing." We don't all like the same music. We are not all musically inclined. To say "Let us sing" is to expose all of our imperfections. When we sing we are guaranteed that we will not perform a perfected masterpiece.

The beauty of our music is not in the precision of our notes but the passion of our hearts. A marvelous list of things to sing about is here: God's greatness; God's vastness; the height of God's goodness; the earth and its beauty and wonder.

And yet as large, powerful, awesome, and good as God is, this God tenderly reminds us that we are the sheep of God's hand. With the provision of the pastures and the love of God's caress, we are blessed indeed.

This is something to sing about.

Secondary Preaching Theme

The Ezekiel passage lends itself to level critique at authorities who rule only by law and not by relationship. A good theme to explore is "I will feed them with justice" (34:16 NRSV). What does that look like and how is that different from merely legislated ideas of justice? How do our self-centered and shortsighted understandings of justice as meted out in human societies pale in comparison? How do we get our human sense of justice to be more aligned with the prophet's vision?

Hymn Suggestions

"He's Got the Whole World in His Hands," Negro Spiritual

"How Great Thou Art," *The United Methodist Hymnal*, 77

"Lift Every Voice and Sing," *The United Methodist Hymnal*, 519

November 26, 2020– Thanksgiving Day

Passages: Deuteronomy 8:7-18; Psalm 65; 2 Corinthians 9:6-15; Luke 17:11-19

Grace Pak

Gathering Prayer

Holy and gracious God, on this day, we gather to glorify you and express our gratitude for your abundant blessings. We thank you for your generosity in giving us all that we are and all that we have. Most of all, we thank you that you did not withhold anything, but gave us your one and only Son Jesus Christ to be our brother, teacher, and savior. May our thanksgiving be more than feelings and words. May our thanksgiving be expressed in our actions and deeds so that your love overflows into the world. May our thanksgiving bring healing to us and our world. We pray in Jesus's name, your greatest gift to us. Amen.

Preaching Theme

When ten men with skin diseases approached Jesus, shouting loudly and asking for healing, Jesus sends them to priests to show themselves, as was the custom, to be declared clean and return to the community. Of the ten, only one returned to Jesus to express his gratitude. Ten men who were in need of healing, when they shouted "Jesus, Master, show us mercy!" showed that they have faith in Jesus. The Samaritan who came back to thank Jesus, shouting praises to God, exhibited deeper faith acknowledging the source of his healing. The first shout asking for mercy resulted in healing that is skin deep. The second shout of praises to God in gratitude brought much deeper healing of the soul. "Your faith has healed you" (v. 19).

There are a few things we learn about thanksgiving from the Samaritan:

- Thanksgiving is raising shouts of praises to God in gratitude for all the blessings we received.

- Thanksgiving is turning back to acknowledge the source of gift.

- Thanksgiving is expressing gratitude "now" and not waiting for the convenient time.

- Thanksgiving is not taking God's gift for granted. As a Samaritan, the man had no reason to expect anything from Jesus, a Jew. He probably felt that he had no right to receive anything, let alone healing.

We give God thanks for everything, for none of us deserve anything from God. We are grateful because there is nothing that came from us. We did not create our own life. We did not give ourselves the family and friends we love and who love us. Every moment we receive is undeserved and unearned, a free gift from God from whom all blessings flow.

Secondary Preaching Theme

After a long forty years of wandering in the wilderness, finally the Israelites are about to cross the Jordan River into the promised land. Moses paints a picture with his words of what they can expect in the new land—the Israelites enjoying prosperity and abundance, satisfaction and blessing. However, Moses warns the Israelites of the spiritual amnesia we are prone to in such environment of comfort and affluence. When we lack nothing and everything is thriving, it is easy to turn away from God. Surrounded and distracted by abundance of things, we forget who we are and whose we are. The antidote to spiritual amnesia is thanksgiving.

Thanksgiving is remembering that God is the source of everything. God is the one who rescued the Israelites from Egypt, from slavery. God is the one who led them through the wilderness, keeping them from all the dangers and harm. God is the one who provided for them throughout the journey, feeding them with manna and making the water gush forth from a rock. God is the one who gives them strength each day for them to enjoy the abundant blessing. Remembering God and giving God thanks is synonymous with keeping God's commands and staying humble. Remembering God is not a passive thought process but an active obedience of commandments. The active remembering of God keeps the people of God connected to and in covenant with God.

Litany of Thanksgiving (with Old 100th Doxology)

We thank you, O Lord God, for your abundant blessings.
Praise God from whom all blessings flow.
We thank you, O Lord God, for your generous gifts of love and joy in our community.
Praise God all creatures here below.
We thank you, O Lord God, for the saving grace and life eternal found in your Son Jesus Christ.
Praise God above all heavenly host.
We thank you, O Lord God, for the call to partner with you in ministry to the world.
Praise Father, Son, and Holy Ghost. Amen.

Offering Prayer

God of abundant blessings, we thank you for providing for all our needs and much more. We have everything we need always, and there is more than enough for every kind of good work. We bring our offerings to express our gratitude for all you gave us. May our offering be the seeds of your grace and mercy that will multiply in many expressions of thanksgiving to you and bring you honor. We thank you for your gifts that words cannot describe! Amen.

Sending Forth

On this Thanksgiving Day, may you raise shouts of praises to God in gratitude for all the blessings you received in the way you are generous to those around you.
On this Thanksgiving Day, may you acknowledge God, the source of all good gifts as you share with those who are in need.
On this Thanksgiving Day, may the peace and joy of Christ overflow extravagantly as your heart is filled with thankfulness.
Amen.

November 29, 2020–First Sunday of Advent

Passages: Isaiah 64:1-9; Psalm 80:1-7, 17-19; 1 Corinthians 1:3-9; Mark 13:24-37

Christopher Heckert

Gathering Prayer

God of light, tear open the clouds and illumine the darkness of human injustice, conflict, and division. Restore our relationships with you and one another through the love of Jesus Christ. May we ready ourselves by letting go of the things that divide us and instead seeing the sacred worth and belatedness of the other. Prepare our hearts to live in your reign that is to come by living into the kingdom that is already upon us. Give us eyes to see, ears to hear, and a heart ready to receive. Amen.

Preaching Theme

Advent begins with anticipation and deep longing for good news on the backdrop of shorter days and longer nights. The common theme in Isaiah and Psalm 80 is a desperate cry for God to show up on the scene and end the period of long suffering. The prophet Isaiah should resonate with current stories of people who live in desolation, despair, and all who are the victims of injustice and oppression. It can seem in these situations that God has hidden God's face and is nowhere to be found.

The Advent cry is for God to tear open the heavens and fix that which is broken, give hope to the downtrodden, and forgive a nation that seemed to have gone astray. Even though Isaiah acknowledges that the distance was initiated by Israel's forsaking God's ways, the prophet is pleading for God's forgiveness and redemption. In the same way, the psalmist offers a litany for God to restore what has been lost and to save God's people from desolation. In Psalm 80, the line "Restore us, God! Make your face shine so that we can be saved" is repeated three times.

From what sins and injustices do we need salvation today as individuals, as a community, and as a society? Let us lift up our own longing for God's healing and redemptive power to shine light even in the darkest of places.

Secondary Preaching Theme

In Mark 13, we see an echo of the cry for help found in Isaiah, but, here, Jesus offers a vision of how God will answer that plea. Here is a clear vision of the Son of Man for the one who belongs to all of humanity, who will return with power to gather and redeem.

But when will this happen? How long, O God, will we have to wait? Jesus's response to such questions is that we must keep alert, be aware, stay awake, and pay attention to the signs of changing seasons. We must look for God all around us and live in God's present reign that creeps up on the margins wherever love changes hearts, redeems brokenness, and saves lives.

Call to Worship

Stay awake, be alert, and pay attention!
God is doing a new thing, and we don't want to miss it!
Wherever there is hurt, pain, brokenness, and injustice,
God is doing a new thing, and we don't want to miss it!
Even though the days are short and the nights seem longer and longer,
God is doing a new thing, and we don't want to miss it!
Like the flickering of a small flame in the middle of the night,
God is doing a new thing, and we don't want to miss it!
Let us worship God who hears our prayer and is doing a new thing! Amen.

Benediction

May God grant you enough light to see the next step moving forward. May God grant peace, that in uncertainty you may find courage. May God grant you love, that in the long journey you may have compassion. Go and be hope for the world! Amen.

December 6, 2020–Second Sunday of Advent

Passages: Isaiah 40:1-11; Psalm 85:1-2, 8-13; 2 Peter 3:8-15a; Mark 1:1-8

Sheila Beckford

Gathering Prayer (Based on Psalm 85:1-2, 8-13 and 2 Peter 3:8-15a)

Merciful God, while we take comfort in experiencing your constant love and affection toward your creation, we often look for a "right now" response to our prayers. And although we turn toward our own resolve and display a lack of faith and trust in you, you remain faithful to us in your response giving us a new found hope in your strength. Forgive us, Lord, for our readiness to return to our foolish ways and lack of understanding. On this second Sunday of Advent, Loving God, help us to always seek ways to find the hope in every situation through your peace, love, guidance, and justice. Help us to walk in your righteous footsteps. Amen.

Preaching Theme

With the decline of church membership across all denominations, many people are scratching their heads and wondering why the church has lost its relevance. We live in a world where the killing of young black children, the caging of brown and black immigrants, violence, oppression, bigotry, hatred, and other ungodly behavior has become more normative than has commitments to refugees, just laws, health care, and saving lives. Simultaneously, too many are experiencing a sense of hopelessness while a wave of "awake movements" and false prophets are on the rise. People are awaiting the return of the Lord and cries of "How long will you forget me, Lord? Forever?" (Ps 13:1) reverberate with every act of injustice.

The first Christians had come to believe that the return of Jesus was imminent. But seventy years passed and no Jesus, no second coming, no restoration of Jerusalem, and no justice. The false teachers argued that the idea of a second coming was ludicrous. They reasoned, "Where is the promise of his coming? After all, nothing has changed—not since the beginning of creation, nor even since the ancestors died" (2 Pet 3:4).

The author warns the believers not to fall into the trap of unbelief or the entanglement of those who did not believe that Jesus would return, thus there would be no judgment. He assures the community that God's promise to return is not based upon their timing, but on God's timing. Furthermore, God's patience is their salvation. Out of all of the 242 characters in this text, these words in verse 15a encapsulated the meaning of this Second Sunday of Advent: "Consider the patience of our Lord to be salvation." God's intentional delay allows or affords more people the gracious opportunity to repent of their lives of bigotry, hatred, oppression, xenophobia, misogyny, and other unjust behavior, in order to escape judgment and begin experiencing the dawn of a new heaven right here on earth. In other words, there is still hope for all of God's people to be redeemed.

God's intentional delay awaits activity from *us*. We too have a responsibility to live the way Jesus lived, challenge the status quo, challenge unjust laws, and provide healing and hope to the world until the long-awaited promise of a new heaven and a new earth where justice reigns is fulfilled.

Secondary Preaching Themes

Throughout the biblical text, the wilderness symbolizes a place where people are destitute, disoriented, divagating, and desperate. In Mark 1, inserted between disoriented and divagating, stands John the Baptist. Through the transformative act of baptism, the community's hearts are turned from a sinful path as he points them toward the way of hope. This is John's stop along this journey because the long-expected messiah—the Chosen One, Human One, Liberator—will lead them out of the wilderness along the path of salvation. The wait will soon be over.

In Isaiah 40, the Israelites find themselves living in a political economy where gentrification, the imposition of higher tax rates, and unfair distribution of wealth caused poverty and oppression. As if that was not enough, their religious freedoms were a thing of the past. This quagmire was self-inflicted. The people rebelled against God, causing a separation between God and them. Isaiah 40:2 suggests that the separation between God and the people was necessary, but it will now come to an end. Unlike the Gospel and the Epistle, the prophet declares that God's intentional delay in responding to their desperation was a punishment and not an act of grace, yet there is hope. God's arms of protection will once again bring the people comfort.

Call to Worship (Based on Isaiah 40:1-11)

We raise our voice and shout, "Messenger!"
Here is our God.
We raise our voices for we are not afraid.
Here is our God.
We find hope in knowing that we are yours, and you are our God. Amen.

Sending Forth

Find comfort in knowing that Christ's delayed return is rooted in love. There is hope for us yet! God is watching and waiting with open arms for all of us to repent. Go into the world sharing the good news that God's saving grace is active in the lives of all people. Amen.

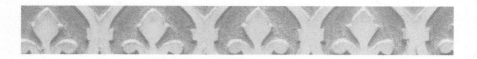

December 13, 2020–Third Sunday of Advent

Passages: Isaiah 61:1-4, 8-11; Luke 1:46b-55; 1 Thessalonians 5:16-24; John 1:6-8

Sudarshana Devadhar

Gathering Prayer

God of all seasons, Holy One, as we light the third candle of Advent in our churches, continue to remind us that you have given us the sacred responsibility of shedding your light in our communities, particularly in places where people live in darkness because of selfishness, greed, anxiety, and fear. Help us, O God, to realize how important it is for us to be your light bearers and grant us the strength and courage to do so no matter the cost. We ask this in the precious name of our Lord and Savior Jesus Christ.

Preaching Themes

Paul offers injunctions for the church (people of God) to be authentic in times of anxiety. His threefold injunctions may serve as great preaching themes.

First, the outward marks of an authentic Christian community include rejoicing always, praying continually, and giving thanks in every situation (1 Thess 5:16-18). Though these may sound anti-cultural or even crazy to a nonbeliever, these are the marks the saints of the church have demonstrated as they relied upon God in their missions and Christian vocations. Second, "Don't suppress the Spirit. Don't brush off Spirit-inspired messages, but examine everything carefully and hang on to what is good" (vv. 19-21). Last, "Avoid every kind of evil" (v. 22). These practices will give you inner strength.

As one develops these themes, it may be fitting to share the witnesses of faithful disciples of Jesus Christ such as Archbishop Oscar Romero, Nelson Mandela, and the Rev. Dr. Martin Luther King Jr.

One of my mentors shared the importance of delivering prophetic, pastoral sermons during the Lenten and Advent seasons. This mentor suggested that during these seasons, people are looking for hope. In my own journey as a pastor, during one Advent season, a parishioner approached me and told me her spouse had quit his job because of the message he received through my sermon. It had been a good job, and he lost some money, but the change allowed him more time for family and other priorities.

Secondary Preaching Themes

The prophet Isaiah reminds us what joyful proclamation looks like! He stresses the role of God's Spirit in our lives. One should also notice that Jesus used Isaiah 61:1-2 as his Nazareth manifesto in Luke 4:16-21. Mary's canticle (Luke 1:46b-55) affirms the faithfulness of God, and how God has shown mercy upon this young woman who was from the margins. We are reminded that John the Baptist "came as a witness to testify concerning the light" (John 1:7).

These secondary themes could be developed into thought-provoking sermons by asking questions such as

- What if every congregation not only read Jesus's Nazareth manifesto but acted upon it in concrete ways?

- What if, during the Advent season, each pastor invited four persons in the congregation to share personal testimonies like Mary's?

- What if every congregation were to have an Advent candle-lighting ceremony and an evening of prayer at which the congregation shared how they have been witnesses for the light of Christ in their own settings, communities, and world?

Responsive Reading (Based on Psalm 126)

When the Lord changed Zion's circumstances for the better,
it was like we had been dreaming.
Our mouths were suddenly filled with laughter;
our tongues were filled with joyful shouts.
It was even said, at that time, among the nations,
"The Lord has done great things for them!"
Yes, the Lord has done great things for us,
and we are overjoyed.
Lord, change our circumstances for the better,
like dry streams in the desert waste!
Let those who plant with tears
reap the harvest with joyful shouts.
Let those who go out,
crying and carrying their seed,
come home with joyful shouts,
carrying bales of grain!

Blessing

May the God of light lead you
to places where there is darkness
that you may shine and reflect the hope and joy of God.
May the God of light fill you with the love of Christ
that your witness may be powerful.

May the God of light hold you
in love and grace forever and ever,

and send you forth in the power of the Holy Spirit. Amen.

December 20, 2020–Fourth Sunday of Advent

Passages: 2 Samuel 7:1-11,16; Luke 1:46b-55; Romans 16:25-27;
Luke 1:26-38

Susan Henry Crowe

Focusing Prayer

"Blessed Be the God of Israel," *The United Methodist Hymnal,* 209

Preaching Theme

Keeping vigil is not only a practice of humans but also of Christian ritual. Keeping vigil in anticipation of birth, sitting with those who are ill, accompanying by their bedsides those who are passing from this life into the next are practices of vigil. We tend to think of vigil with death, but grandmothers and grandfathers know ever so well vigil keeping as their first, second or third grandchild is being born. The night is long, the mother is exhausted, the hospital is cold, and coffee is hard to find and yet this longest night is never forgotten. The joy that comes is unspeakable.

Every young mother to be is full of wonder, curiosity and sometimes fear about this experience of carrying life and giving birth. She knows that her Mother, aunties, sisters, friends who carried their babies before, hold the secrets of wisdom which convey, the mystery, the power and the hope, the joy of this journey. In the statue of Mary and Elizabeth we see the myriad expressions of wonder, companionship, wisdom, and curiosity, all joined in the mysteries of birth. The expected is not what is to come.

The journey to the manger must have been full exhaustion, uncertainty, setbacks, unexpected friendships, and being turned away at the end of the journey. And yet the presence of God is there—reminding that God is ever present on the journey of giving birth, holding close a family, showing the way into life and the world that is yet to come.

Yahweh reminds David through Nathan in 2 Samuel, "I've been with you wherever you have gone." In David's case it is from the pasture into a different kind of kingship with the reminder that Yahweh has not been in a cedar temple but traveling in a tent and in a dwelling. The assurance is that Yahweh is always with us wherever we go. Yahweh's presence is the forerunner and the antecedent of Emmanuel, God, ever present, with us.

These texts are those of vigils kept and hope delivered as well as giving a nod to what is to come. The dangers and joys of birth are a precursor of the Lenten journey pointing to the Easter vigil—keeping watch for life.

Worship Helps

Visual suggestion: "The Visitation" by Luca della Robbia

Antiphonal reading suggestion: "Our Lady of the New Advent, Burning Bush" by Mirabai Starr

Readings

2 Samuel 7:1-11, 16: Nathan's vision to David, "I've been with you wherever you have gone."

Luke 1:46b-55: Sung Reading, "Tell Out, My Soul," *The United Methodist Hymnal*, 200

Romans 16:25-27: Final Prayer from Paul to the Church at Rome
Luke 1:26-38: Jesus's birth foretold

December 24, 2020– Christmas Eve

Passages: Isaiah 9:2-7; Psalm 96; Titus 2:11-14; Luke 2:1-14 [15-20]

LaTrelle Easterling

Opening Prayer

Glorious God, in the beauty of holiness we await the coming of your Son. A people who walked in darkness have seen a great light. Through the seed of David and nurtured in the womb of Mary, you sent a glorious hope to break forth upon the horizon. The light of truth pierces all that is untrue. The light of justice breaks through the clouds of injustice. The light of mercy outshines the darkness of despair. In the stillness we await your Light, Holy God—that Light is Jesus: Wonderful Counselor, Mighty God, Eternal Creator, the Prince of Peace! Come, Lord Jesus, come. We have made room for you.

Preaching Theme

Isaiah stands as a testament to the blessing of unwavering faith. It is a story told through the metaphors of darkness and light. The poetic story espouses a knowing beyond knowing that God is in control and will ultimately provide. It is neither a Pollyannaish naivete nor an eschatological hope resigned to present futility. Rather, these verses offer a full-throated belief that the Lord is light and that light brings deliverance. The writer of Isaiah understood the incredible yearning for freedom that burns in the heart of the oppressed. As a people living under the threat of wars from tyrannical kings, the people of Judah needed a king with integrity and deep faith. Their former leader, Ahaz, was felled by fear and soiled by corruption. His reign lived into the words of Lord Acton: "Power tends to corrupt, and absolute power corrupts absolutely." How have leaders without integrity hurt the kin-dom of God today? Where do we see abuse of the vulnerable?

Through this birth, God is breaking into history to save, protect, and comfort God's people. These verses should impart courage as the Light promises defeat of strongholds and foes. Christ-followers should have no fear in calling for justice. If we believe in this light, are we compelled to join God in shining a light wherever darkness lurks? What do Christ-followers say of God's witness in Isaiah when we fail to stand against oppression?

The strength of the light in this pericope also informs the personal life of the believer. The power of the light is strong enough to sustain believers even during a dark night of the soul. What testimony can we offer of trusting in God when all seemed lost?

Secondary Preaching Themes

Caesar Augustus was hailed as a ruler who brought peace. However, as the biblical narrative demonstrates, reliance on political rulers often leads to disappointment. The good news of Luke is that while Caesar rules through worldly means, the Savior comes with all power in his hands. Do we rely solely on God for our needs? Even though Augustus was associated with peace, the people still lived under Roman rule. The birth announcement of Christ the Lord, from the royal lineage of David, brings the assurance of divine intervention and hope for a lasting peace. The announcement is made not through human means, but by heavenly ambassadors, further evidencing a divine hand. In situating the announcement this way, there is a mystical nature to the birth of Christ. Have we left room for mystery in our worship of Christ the King? The Lukan narrative assures us that this announcement is good news for *all* people. Do we live the birth of Christ so as ensure it is good news for all?

In the midst of our celebrations and merriment, precipitated by the Gregorian and the liturgical calendar, the words of Titus should stop us in our tracks. It causes us to pause and transition from an outward focus to an inward reflection. The words of Titus introduce personal responsibility and accountability to the receiving of God's gift. It also moves us beyond an easier focus on Christ as an infant to the remembrance of Christ on the cross, and the gift of eternal life we've been given. How can we both celebrate the birth of Christ and recognize his larger messianic message?

Responsive Reading

Sing to the Lord a new song! Sing to the Lord all the earth.
Declare God's glory among the nations; declare his wondrous works among all peoples.
The Lord is great and greatly to be praised. The Lord who created heaven and earth.
Declare God's glory among the nations; declare his wondrous works among all peoples.
Bring gifts to the God of gods; enter his courtyard with exultations.
Declare God's glory among the nations; declare his wondrous works among all peoples.
The Lord rules with fairness and equity. Even the trees of the earth rejoice at his judgment.
Hallelujah! The Lord establishes justice. Hallelujah! The Lord has brought justice for all!

December 25, 2020– Christmas Day

Passages: Isaiah 62:6-12; Psalm 97; Titus 3:4-7; Luke 2:1-7, 8-20

Alisha Gordon

Gathering Prayer

Holy one, born in a manger, we seek you on this day we acknowledge the day of your birth. Through heaven's gates you came to us in a lowly manger, a place fit for animals, so that all may begin to see both God's justice and grace in human form. May we always declare and share your goodness with all who will listen, for it is in our sharing that we find peace, joy, and encouragement.

Preaching Theme

"Go tell it on the mountain, over the hills and everywhere," the African American spiritual proclaims. The shepherds in Luke 2:8-20 were compelled by the need to not only "go tell it" but to "go see it" for themselves. As they laid watch over their sheep, they received a divine word that Jesus Christ was born—a divine word that compelled them to travel for miles to see for themselves what they had heard. And when they arrived, they retold the story of what the angels told them and "everyone who heard it was amazed at what the shepherds told them" (v. 18). What word has God put into your spirit that compels you to go see for yourself? How does the sharing of the good news shift the experiences of those who care to hear it. Sharing good news is contagious!

Secondary Preaching Themes

In Isaiah 62:6-12, we see again how proclamation and the sharing of what God has done compels the people into preparation and thanksgiving. The people of Israel are busying themselves with preparing the way of the Lord because of God's promise to establish Jerusalem, to return them back to a place of joy and restoration. Too often we lose our zeal to make room or prepare for what is to come because we are focused on what once was. This scripture encourages us to not rest until we see God do what God has promised—and God is sure to make good on God's promises.

In Titus 3:4-7, we are reminded that God's mercy toward us is not contingent upon what we do. God's mercy is because of God's reverberating love for us. Even when we are unkind, disobedient, or selfish, God sees the best in us and pours out her love on us so both what we say and what we do is reflective of the gift of grace.

Congregational Moment

Invite congregants to share a bit of good news with one another as a form of welcome or passing the peace.

Song of Worship/Response

Psalm 97, *The United Methodist Hymnal*

Benediction (Based on Psalm 97)

Now to the Lord who rules and calls for rejoicing, to the God whose heavens have proclaimed God's righteousness and glory, let us go forth as Zion and Judah and celebrate, rejoice, and revel in your acts of justice. We give thanks today and forevermore. Amen.

December 27, 2020

Passages: Isaiah 61:10–62:3; Psalm 148; Galatians 4:4-7; Luke 2:22-40

Jennifer and Todd Pick

Gathering Prayer

God of Light and Life, we join with all creation in singing songs of praise and celebration! You call us to see beyond human sight, to behold the good news of your promises faithfully fulfilled. As strains of "Christ the Savior is born" still echo, we lift our voices to sing of a world transformed by your love, born in us anew.

Preaching Theme

The season of Christmas is filled with some of the most beloved songs in the Christian tradition. These "modern" carols lend their voices to the angel chorus that sang in the Christ child's birth to lowly shepherds in the Lukan Gospel. Forty days have passed since heavenly forces sang, and Jesus is brought to the temple in accordance with the Law of Moses. We wonder if the angels' song still echoed in the air as we first meet Simeon. We wonder if, in waiting for the promised one who would restore Israel, he heard strains of the angelic chorus blending with God's song in his heart. Did he hear the prophet Isaiah's refrains of light coming back into the world? Did he hear Mary echoing Hannah's song of justice, where the powerful are brought down from their thrones and the lowly are lifted? Did the song grow louder as Jesus was brought into the temple that day? Over a lifetime, Simeon must have witnessed many children brought to the temple to be dedicated, but this day was different. Led by the Spirit, he saw Jesus and couldn't wait to hold salvation in his arms!

Praising God, Simeon offers a bittersweet melody of letting go. His eyes have seen God's promise fulfilled, and he knows that there will be a new refrain sung—not only for Israel, but for the nations (Gentiles) as well. He knows that there will be someone to carry God's song after he is gone. A joyful sadness fills the air as he tells Mary that a sorrow, like a piercing sword, will one day break her heart.

Perhaps the prophet Anna overheard Simeon's song of blessing or was drawn by the same Spirit that moved him to the Christ child. She adds her own voice to the growing song, praising God. Luke gives her (and curiously not Simeon) the distinction of being *a prophet*. This means she has eyes to see what others do not and to speak about what she sees with words of hope. Anna confirms that this child will bring freedom and release to God's people. Both she and Simeon have waited faithfully and patiently. They are both fully present to this moment of revelation, this moment of meeting salvation in-the-flesh. Acknowledging a deeper reality than can be seen, they begin to sing.

And when we can see and know the deeper reality that this Child of Life represents a light stronger than darkness, hope stronger than despair, love stronger than death, we respond by joining in the song of salvation!

Secondary Preaching Theme

As we read all the lectionary texts for this first Sunday of Christmas, there is a chorus praising God. In Isaiah, there is an exuberant song of joy and victory. "I won't keep silent....I won't sit still." (62:1) It seems the prophet is not only singing, but dancing as well. A new name is also given, just as Jesus is named in the temple. The psalmist also recalls that all creation, including the stars, sea monsters, and every single cedar, joins in the heavenly chorus of singing praise to God. Nothing on earth should be silent. The Galatians text echoes Luke in speaking about the fulfilment of the Law. It also draws on the theme of the nations (Gentiles) being adopted into the family of God, just as Simeon sang that the Christ would be a light to the nations.

Responsive Reading

We pause in wonder at God's love born among us.
With eyes that see salvation, we cradle the Child of Light!
We welcome God's presence revealed to us!
With voices that sing praise, we greet the Child of Blessing!
We walk without fear as God's peace enfolds us.
With hearts that hold good news, we carry the Child of Promise!
Come, carry the light! Come, sing songs of blessing!
Come, celebrate the promise of God With Us!

Benediction

Bright stars, stormy winds, and ocean depths sing to you, Source of Life. With the trees and birds and all creatures great and small, we add our voices to the song of praise. As we recognize your light in the darkness, sing in us a new vision for your creation. As we give voice to your lifesaving love among us, give us eyes to see heaven and earth joined as one. Set your Spirit in our hearts until they beat to the rhythm of your blessing. Open our ears to the melody of your peace until we are singing it with our lives. Let our songs of praise accompany actions that bring about your justice and your peace. Amen.

A Case for Homiletic Empathy

Excerpt from *Preaching with Empathy*
by Lenny Luchetti

Finding a universally accepted definition of empathy can be as difficult as locating Bigfoot or spotting a unicorn. Still, let's consider a few possible definitions. Empathy is "an imaginative endeavor that results in us having the same type of feeling or emotion as the other person";[1] "the capacity to think and feel oneself into the inner life of another person";[2] or "an affective response more appropriate to another's situation than one's own."[3] However, Roman Krznaric's definition may be most helpful because it includes affective, cognitive, and behavioral dynamics. He writes, "empathy is the art of stepping imaginatively into the shoes of another person, understanding their feelings and perspectives, and using that understanding to guide your actions."[4] Empathy is the skill and, I contend, the grace that bridges the gap of distance between my reality and another's.

What does empathy have to do with preaching? Everything. Homiletic empathy is the grace that enables preachers to imagine their way into the situational shoes of others, to understand the thoughts and feel the emotions of listeners. Only then can they preach in a manner most responsive to their listeners' deepest needs. Homiletic empathy bridges the chasm between the preacher and the ethnically, generationally, educationally, economically, geographically, and spiritually diverse people to whom he or she preaches. Empathy turns a Bible study into a sermon. Empathy transforms information into impact. Empathy enables intimacy between pulpit and pew. Yes, empathy matters!

Homiletic empathy is easier to describe than define. An old man in his seventies came to preach at a Christian college where I served as pastor. When I picked him up at the airport, I immediately felt sorry for the guy. I imagined students would nap through his sermon series. There was a huge gap of distance between this seventy-year-old brilliant Old Testament scholar and these eighteen-to twenty-two-year-olds, half of whom had no idea Zephaniah is a book in the Bible. Yet, despite the fact that he didn't sport a goatee, tattoos, or skinny jeans, he connected with students on a profound level. The impact of his words upon their lives surprised me and, I think, the students. I recall him voicing the doubts, hopes, and fears of college students with contextual precision, as if he himself were one of them. What did the late Dr. Dennis Kinlaw have that enabled his sermonic words to bridge the generational and educational gap between himself and his collegiate listeners? Empathy!

Safiyah was a well-educated African American woman in her thirties, appointed by her bishop to pastor a church in Iowa full of white rural folks, farmers mostly. Her education, ethnicity, and upbringing did not at all match the congregational demographics. This was the kind of "match" that makes us ponder what, or if, the bishop was thinking. Yet her preaching connected, and the church grew. How was the ethnic and geographic chasm overcome? Empathy!

Donovan is Caucasian, born and raised in the rural Midwest. He has been pastoring a church in urban Jersey City, New Jersey, for more than four decades. During most of his ministry there, he and his family have been the only white people in the church. His African American and Caribbean black congregants love him because he has found a way to articulate their dreams and disappointments for them through his preaching. What does Donovan have that allows him to leap the tall cultural fence between him and his congregants? Empathy!

I was a twenty-three-year-old college senior called to pastor a church in which the average age in the congregation was like 125. That's a stretch, but not much. I am an urbanite, born and bred in Philadelphia. That church was full of retirees from Podunk who had been following Christ three times longer than I had been alive. We could not be more dissimilar. Hard homiletic questions hounded me. How can I get past the naive nose on my face and jump into the scuffed-up pointy-toed shoes and bib overalls of senior men and the flowery dresses and knee-high stockings of elderly women? How can I articulate words that reflect not merely my preferences and perspectives but their particular thoughts and feelings? How in the name of Lawrence Welk and Johnny Carson can I put the gospel in a contextual container from which they can drink? Empathy!

In a cultural context of anger and apathy that results in callousness, a context in which the church has lost her power and privilege, how does the Christian preacher get a hearing? The present age demands not only exegesis or eloquence but empathy. The preacher who embodies with words and manner, in content and delivery, the empathy of God for the human race (chapter 3) will preach with amplified power. Empathy makes the homiletical world go 'round. But how much does empathy matter to preachers?

Though empathy is arguably the most important disposition necessary for fruitful preaching today, it seems to be flying under the radar of preachers who are on the prowl for skill development. There is, to my knowledge, no book written on the topic of preaching with empathy, which is why I wrote this one. I could only find a handful of book chapters or academic papers that name the topic at all. Empathy is a needle in the homiletic haystack for which only a few seem to be looking.

Not long ago, I conducted a brief survey on Facebook and Twitter. I asked the pastors among my friends and followers to respond to this question: What are the two or three most important skills necessary for preaching today? There were fifty-eight respondents. One of them replied, "Great hair and skinny jeans." Not the most helpful response. Only six of the fifty-eight respondents specifically cited empathy. That's only ten percent. In all, 139 skills were mentioned. Only twelve of the 139 had any resemblance to empathy. That's only 8.6 percent. Clearly, empathy is not high on the list of preaching priorities. Without it, however, preaching falls flat.

APATHY		EMPATHY
Callous: does not feel concern for others	Affective	Passionate: feels concern for others
Disinterested: does not care to know the needs and perspectives of others	Cognitive	Curious: seeks to know the needs and perspectives of others
Passive: does not respond to the needs of others	Behavioral	Active: responds to the needs of others

This excerpt, "A Case for Homiletic Empathy" by Lenny Luchetti, is from *Preaching with Empathy: Crafting Sermons in a Callous Culture*, in The Artistry of Preaching Series (Nashville: Abingdon Press, 2019).

Preaching to Millennials[1]

Excerpt from *Say Something!*
by Charley Reeb

Millennials (those between the ages of eighteen and thirty-four) are notoriously known to be skeptical of faith and the church. We have heard the reasons: "Millennials feel entitled and lack a sense of commitment"; "Many millennials did not grow up in the church and don't see the value in institutions like the church"; "Millennials don't feel the church does enough to address social problems"; "Millennials reject the church because of the self-righteous Christians they have known."

While I would not argue that there is some truth to these sweeping statements, there may be a simpler reason why many millennials are not in the pews: the sermon. The hard truth is that most sermons don't connect with millennials. I did some research on the millennials I know and asked them about how they listen to sermons. Based on the feedback I received, there are three things a sermon much accomplish in order to reach millennials:

1. Validate their skepticism.

One of the biggest reasons why many millennials don't feel comfortable in churches is because they feel their skepticism is not welcome. Sermons that resonate with millennials validate their doubts and questions of faith. Be willing to share your own struggles with doubt and faith and what they taught you. Also, don't assume all of your listeners are Christians. Consider the possibility that there will be atheists, agnostics, and other curious people in attendance and acknowledge them in your sermon. Quite often in my sermons I will say, "Perhaps you are not a Christian and have come to worship because you are curious about Christianity. You are always welcome here." Don't underestimate the power of making such a statement in your sermon. Validate skepticism and acknowledge the curious and your sermons will go a long way for millennials.

2. Answer the "Yeah, but...."

Millennials have all information in the world in their pocket. Whenever you reference a passage of scripture or use a sermon illustration they can take out their phones and Google it. In seconds they can know whether your illustration is true (or your own!) and can read other articles and sermons on your text. The result is that millennials know all the angles and can present an argument against what you are saying. The lesson: Do your homework! Consider questions and counterarguments to your sermons and answer them. "Some of you may be thinking, yeah but . . ." You gain a great deal of credibility with millennials when they sense you have done your research and anticipate the questions they will be asking.

3. Share why faith is important.

Millennials, more than any other generation, embrace the variety of entertainment and stimulation in our culture today. They are keenly aware of the myriad of ways they can spend their time. Therefore, sermons must not only be compelling but also convince them why investing time in matters of faith is important. Why should they have a relationship with God? Why should they read the Bible? Why should they pray? Why should they join a small group? Why should they attend worship on a regular basis? Why should they serve others? Many millennials did not grow up in church and don't know why taking a break from social media to read the Bible and pray is important. Don't assume they know why.

This excerpt, "Preaching to Millennials" by Charley Reeb, is from *Say Something! Simple Ways to Make Your Sermons Matter* (Nashville: Abingdon Press, 2019).

Soul Wounds in the Church

Excerpt from *Words That Heal*
by Joni S. Sancken

In a book that focuses on how the church and preaching in particular can be a part of God's healing of traumatic wounds, we must look at wounds the church has at times inadvertently inflicted upon others. Preaching can be an integral part of facilitating healing for the church and for those harmed by the church's actions or inactions. A strong leader can help individuals and groups move toward healing by helping survivors feel safe; by disrupting corrupt, abusive, or violent cycles; and by gathering groups of support within a congregation.[1] Sermons can actively support these ministries.

The church has caused and deepened wounds in a variety of ways. A church leader with gifts for ministry can simultaneously be deeply broken and act in sinful, illegal, and wounding ways. The church has also acted collectively in ways that have wounded individuals and groups. Racism, sexism, colonialism, participation in cultural genocide, anti-Semitism, and complicity in the face of clergy sexual abuse are examples of traumatic wounds caused in part by or deepened by the church. God has redeemed the church as the body of Christ, but congregations are still comprised of people and are subject to the promise and peril associated with being human.

Actions that harm another also create a reciprocal wound in the perpetrator, linking both groups in a painful dance. While these wounds might not impact every church member directly, the church's corporate witness has been hurt by wounding behaviors that have recently come to light. In past generations, people may have automatically trusted a member of the clergy. This is no longer the case. Recent decades have brought scandals surrounding clergy sexual abuse across most denominations. Systemic cover-ups are well known, highlighted in the Netflix series *The Keepers* and Oscar-winning film *Spotlight*. Denominations have negotiated legal and financial settlements associated with abuse and cultural trauma caused to indigenous peoples, and megachurch pastors have been charged with financial mismanagement and fraud.

Trauma is a wound that threatens the ability of an organism to function; God offers the church healing and the opportunity to be a witness to God's love in a wounded world. Our Christian witness is unified and strengthened when we face our collective wounding behaviors, change practices, and seek forgiveness. The scars that remain can serve as generative reminders, much like the scars on the hands and feet of the crucified and risen Christ.

Some in our congregations may feel a desire for justice for survivors of wounds caused or deepened by the church leaders or structures, while others resist acknowledging these wounds and simply want to move forward. Being in relationship with those who carry wounds from trauma is difficult. It can be draining and time-consuming. It can be painful for pastors—who love the church and who have given their lives to its service—to learn about the damage that other congregations, church structures, past practices, or leaders have caused. While it can be complex to walk alongside those with soul wounds connected to the church, God's justice and sanctifying grace urge us on.

This chapter explores how the church has caused or contributed to traumatic wounds and offers suggestions for preachers seeking to support healing. As with the other chapters, principles offered here may be useful to preaching that fosters healing for many experiences of pain and brokenness and for pastors who desire to be sensitive to the needs of diverse listeners. What makes this chapter different is attention to the dynamics present when the church has contributed to or deepened a traumatic wound. While the church has contributed to a range of wounds, the issue of sexual abuse in the church has been particularly shrouded in shame and has not been effectively addressed in regular congregational worship contexts. In a recent entry on Our Stories Untold, a website oriented around support for survivors, one of the moderators discusses the challenges facing survivors and communities of faith:

> The other day, my colleagues and I were reflecting on the sense of angst we have when folks in communities of faith ask us for examples of people getting it right when it comes to responding to abuse....The problem is, we don't know of many success stories to tell. Partly, that's because they're shockingly uncommon. In my years of talking and hanging out and working with survivors of sexual violence, I can count on one hand the number who have been satisfied with the way their reports of violence were handled. Just kidding! I can count them on no hands, because zero is the number of sexual violence survivors who have ever said to me anything remotely close to that.[2]

Using the wound of sexual abuse in the church as an example that could be applied to other wounding situations, I will explore resistance often expressed by congregations and church institutions in addressing wounds. The discussion will then turn to specific dynamics associated with the wound of sexual abuse in the church and options for preachers that address these dynamics in order to facilitate God's healing for the church and survivors. A sample sermon demonstrates one attempt to put these techniques to work.

While the wound of sexual abuse is raised as an example here, the preaching suggestions are applicable to any situation where the church at some level has acknowledged its role in causing or intensifying soul wounds. Preaching that supports healing from wounds related to the church is usually most fruitful when the preacher has some support from other leaders either in the congregation or in broader denominational structures.

This excerpt, "Soul Wounds in the Church" by Joni S. Sancken, is from *Words That Heal: Preaching Hope to Wounded Souls* in The Artistry of Preaching Series (Nashville: Abingdon Press, 2019).

What Preaching Does Best

Excerpt from *Practicing the Preaching Life*
by David B. Ward

When someone finally discerns what she does best, that person usually uncovers her own truest longing. Until then we are often Martha, worried and distracted by many things. When a minister focuses her life according to a true and deep longing, it is hard to overestimate how much good she can accomplish. Preaching is often like the gifted minister. Preaching has too many possibilities to pursue, too many requests and aims from outsiders. If preaching is pressed to do everything it can do, it will crumple under the weight of seeking to please too many masters. In order to define and limit the expectations on preachers and preaching, this chapter will explore the preacher's longing and define the preacher's doing. The next chapter will sketch the preacher's way of being.

The good preacher's longing is shaped by the aim of preaching. The good preacher's doing is guided by the functions of preaching. The good preacher's being is characterized by the contextual virtues of preaching. The preacher's longing, doing, and being are what make a preacher truly good. When these are out of order, even though preaching skills are in place, a preacher is not truly good even if he is excellent. When a preacher is short on preaching skills, but these things are in order, they may be truly called "good" in the most important sense of the term. Great preachers are both good and excellent at the same time.

It is not our doing that first drives us toward better preaching. It is our *longing*. A misdirected longing is like a dog left alone who eagerly devours a neglected candy bar. The misdirected longing brings short-term pleasure and long-term misery. For many preachers do not realize the misery they experience is the result of their longing. If a preacher misunderstands what preaching does best, that preacher may miss the beauty of the preaching life. Burnout, compassion fatigue, and perfectionism among other things can consume the preacher's joy.

Our task in this chapter is to consider the historic wisdom regarding what preaching does best. When preachers recognize what preaching does best and how it does it best, they can reorient their longings for preaching accordingly. Perhaps it will help to begin our exploration of the preacher's longing by listing desires that might mislead us into thinking they are the aim of preaching.

The aim of preaching is not a good sermon.

The aim of preaching is not a successful ministry.

The aim of preaching is not the respect of our community or peers.

The aim of preaching is not the chance to preach in more prestigious places.

The aim of preaching is not to be perceived as spiritual or holy.

The aim of preaching is not to save souls.

The aim of preaching is not to teach doctrine.

The aim of preaching is not to heal hearts.

The aim of preaching is not to undo unjust wrongs.

The aim of preaching is not to tear down oppressive structures.

Certainly, some of the above are greater and nobler than others, but all fall short of the glory of what preaching has aimed for across the ages. All of these things are too small for preaching and too short a vision for the preacher's heart. Each of these desires, even the ones that are twisted toward selfish ends, has something to do with the aim of preaching but is not the aim itself. If we want to practice the preaching life we must aim that life in the right direction and order our longings according to our aim. Preachers need to aim at the right end and hope to achieve it.

This excerpt, "What Preaching Does Best" by David B. Ward, is from *Practicing the Preaching Life* (Nashville: Abingdon Press, 2019).

Modern and Internet Ages: The Social Context of Preaching

Excerpt from *The Four Pages of the Sermon, Revised and Updated* by Paul Scott Wilson

Perhaps it is no coincidence that in the same years that Western culture was transitioning to digital media, it also was also completing a transition from modern to postmodern attitudes. There may be no better symbol of postmodernism than the internet. While the term "postmodernism" is already somewhat out of fashion on the runways of philosophical thought, for new generations of Christians, *postmodernity*—for lack of a better term—is a norm. It affects everyone in Western society, even if they have not heard of it. It is around us and in us, like it or not. It is part of the larger landscape, as James K. A. Smith argued in his *Who's Afraid of Postmodernism?*[1] and I have argued in *Preaching as Poetry: Beauty, Goodness and Truth in Every Sermon*.[2]

Much in the postmodern world arose as a healthy reaction to modernity's perceived excessive trust in reason. Minority groups were seen to be harmed or silenced by the imposition of modernity's standards of unity and conformity. Postmodernity is characterized by suspicion and questioning, disunity and diversity, and interlinking systems and networks. The internet is an excellent symbol of postmodernism; it demonstrates much postmodern theory. Single overarching metanarratives, like the American dream, are rejected by some scholars in favor of individual stories that do not fit into a neat pattern. Texts and symbols are recognized to be multivalent, having various possible interpretations, depending on one's perspective. Horizontal authority, shared control, decentralization, and transparency are trusted more than vertical, centralized models. Ongoing conversation is valued over fixed conclusions, answers, and closure. Communication and process are valued over product and goal. Relativism tends to rule. Some people say there is no truth, only interpretations of it, or that truth is historically and culturally specific. Truth and reality themselves are suspect by many.

The Internet age, postmodernity, or other related concepts (metamodern, post-postmodern, post-secular, post-Christian, post-truth, post-fact) cannot be ignored because the realities to which they point are in the culture at large, in the people who come to church, and in each preacher in complex subtle and non-subtle ways. Nonetheless, some understandings associated with postmodern philosophy are contrary to Christian teaching:

Christians affirm truth, known most plainly in Jesus Christ ("you will know the truth, and the truth will set you free," John 8:32), even if reality is apprehended, as Paul said, "through a glass, darkly" (1 Cor 13:12 KJV).

What one person or group thinks is good, others may not, but true goodness is not merely relative, and "every good gift…is from above" (James 1:17 KJV). The overarching Christian story is necessarily a metanarrative (i.e., one umbrella story of God's love that includes all), but the Bible is also what critics demand: many individual stories (i.e., biblical books and individual preaching texts) that allow for various individual and communal perspectives.

Dramatic shifts have taken place in culture in recent decades as modern values have given way to alternative perspectives. For a few decades "postmodern" was used to describe what came after the modern, but this term too has been challenged, for several reasons: (1) it implied a unified or coherent ideology, when in fact the current age has many competing and divergent understandings and no core program. No one term adequately captures the diverging views. (2) Postmodernism was associated with taking things apart, finding inner contradictions, or deconstruction not reconstruction. Philosophers and critics looked for how authors undermined their own arguments with their own words. A civil rights argument might be dismissed because its author could be interpreted to deny rights to others. An essay might be rejected for presenting binary alternatives, seeming to deny other legitimate alternatives. (3) Postmodern thought could lead to absurdity and anarchy.[3] No argument could withstand its microscopic search for vulnerabilities. Truth and goodness seemed to depend on anyone's perspective and any authority could be undermined. (4) Postmodernity never found traction in large sections of human activity, like in practical science and mathematics, investment banking, or in most non-Western cultures. In these contexts, values associated with the modern often continue to govern.

The realities to which postmodernity points cannot simply be ignored however. What is good about the term "postmodern" is that it clearly marks the current era as after the modern, contrasting with the modern, and as significant as the modern in terms of a paradigm. The ways of thinking that characterize the internet age are not going away. The social realities to which the various terms point may well help shape the next century as we move toward a technological future no one can predict. Whatever has been opened is not going back in the box.

Much of contemporary society looks modern, particularly in traditional communities, and much looks postmodern. It is tempting to identify propositional preaching with the modern era out of which it arose: it tends toward vertical notions of authority, reducing texts to concepts, arguing to a conclusion, single truths, and so on. And it is tempting to identify the New Homiletic with postmodernity. It tends to trust: horizontal notions of authority; texts having many meanings, not just one; reading texts with suspicion; interpretation arising out of and addressing specific contexts, not the generalized human condition, and so on. Still, neither mode of preaching is exclusively one or the other, and the gospel stands over against both modern and postmodern culture—over culture in general. Modernity and reason will not finally save and neither will postmodernity, communication, and suspicion. Both need critical assessment and engagement.

The internet also affects how people receive preaching. The present age seems more focused on the future, on what will come next. History is passé in both senses, concerned with the past and out of fashion. For many people today, a faith that is rooted in events two thousand years ago seems antique, if not obsolete. One-size-fits-all worship is not inviting for many.[4] People want information in relatively short packages. They want it to be practical, of immediate relevance for their lives. Sermon forms need to accommodate shorter attention spans. Preachers feel pressure to use digital technology to accompany the sermon, and churches spend large amounts of money on computers, screens, monitors, and other equipment.

Through history, artists have sought to render the Bible visually, and many great paintings of biblical texts are not only sermons in themselves, they can also be used in sermons. In the past, church bulletins and banners were sometimes used to supply visuals for sermons. The use of video clips and digital images in our own time is a variation on this. There is no shortage of video material available to use: finding it, editing it, and getting it to work flawlessly is time consuming, however, and technology may not yet be sufficiently advanced to streamline the process.

Preachers using audiovisual technology may draw some lessons from the advent of narrative with the New Homiletic. The goal for the sermon is not one long story, or one long video show. Story and video are tools to communicate reality. They do not replace the need for propositional discourse. Stories and videos need theological purpose and interpretation. A clear organizational structure and a single theme for the sermon are still essential. Some stories and images can be too powerful and should be avoided, like those presenting evil and violence, though both need to be acknowledged realities. Use of narrative and video technology is neither good nor bad, it is the purposes to which they are put, and their effectiveness as tools of the gospel, that need to be assessed.

Additional guidelines in using audiovisuals may apply:

- Recruit young people to help with sermon technology; it can give them an important ministry in service of preaching.

- Move sermon preparation time forward in the week so that technical people can participate in helping find the right images.

- Keep video clips short. Don't try to show a long section of a movie, just a brief portion is sufficient, perhaps no longer than one or two minutes.

- The words of the sermon take priority over the visuals. Determine the heart of the sermon's message before looking for audiovisual accompaniment.

- Do not feel pressured to have more than one image on a screen for the sermon. Let preparation time be a key determinant in the number and kind of images you use.

- Beware of compliments about visual technology. People may like a video clip for reasons other than service of the gospel.

- Resist using video to entertain: at best, a sermon with video is a narrated documentary—a modest genre. The church need not try to compete with the entertainment industry.

Some cautions against use of audiovisuals are also appropriate:

- The sermon is not just another video production. People need a Word from God, not more time in front of a digital screen.

- Preachers who favor video underestimate the power of well-crafted words on their own to create pictures and to enroll people in stories that "happen" through the sermon.

- Sermons without videos are typically evaluated negatively by what they often have been (i.e., trouble), not what they can be when they proclaim the gospel (as is the overall purpose here to demonstrate).

- Audiovisual clips are powerful—Marshall McLuhan called them a hot medium, and speech a cool one—and can shift the center of gravity in a sermon. People can be disappointed when a video clip ends and the preacher returns to speech that by comparison may seem dull and lifeless.

- The center of gravity can shift to eclipse the office of the pastor. The preacher can become perceived as a narrator, or lecturer, or entertainer, not the one who ministers care for the people.

- The center of gravity can shift to eclipse the office of proclaimer. When the pastoral office is reduced, so is the capacity of the preacher to speak on behalf of God the liberating words of the gospel.

- Preachers may favor technology over the hard work and power of preaching the gospel. Use of technology should only be contemplated if the words of the sermon stand on their own.

This excerpt, "Modern and Internet Ages: The Social Context of Preaching" by Paul Scott Wilson, is from *The Four Pages of the Sermon, Revised and Updated: A Guide to Biblical Preaching* (Nashville: Abingdon Press, 2018).

Notes

Editor's Introduction

1. C. Michael Hawn, "History of Hymns: 'Come Sunday' Reflects Duke Ellington's Faith & Sacred Jazz Tradition," The United Methodist Church, www.umcdiscipleship.org/resources/history-of-hymns-come-sunday-reflects.

January

1. Eleanor Beardsley, "Off the Record: A Quest for De-Baptism in France," NPR, January 29, 2012, www.npr.org/2012/01/29/146046428/on-the-record-a-quest-for-de-baptism-in-france.

2. For a starting point on this discussion, see: Gary V. Simpson, "Gender, Race and Ethnicity" in *The New Interpreter's Handbook on Preaching.* (Nashville, AbingtonPress, 2008), 269–272.

February

1. Rodney Stark, *The Rise of Christianity* (Princeton, NJ: Princeton University Press, 1996), 82.

March

1. Stephanie Farr and Sam Wood, "A Hidden Hellscape," *Philadelphia Inquirer,* February 19, 2017, www.philly.com/philly/health/addiction/A_hidden_heroin_hellscape.html.

2. Albert Einstein College of Medicine, "Built-in 'Self-Destruct Timer' Causes Ultimate Death of Messenger RNA in Cells," *Science Daily,* December 22, 2011, www.sciencedaily.com/releases/2011/12/111222133454.htm.

3. "Hold Fast" Lyrics © Laurie Zelman, September 2018. Permission granted to use for worship. This song is arranged to the tune of the African American spiritual "Go Down, Moses" in *The United Methodist Hymnal,* 448.

May

1. See Marcus J. Borg, *Speaking Christian: Why Christian Words Have Lost Their Meaning and Power—and How They Can Be Restored* (New York: Harper-Collins, 2012).

2. The literary reference to "a dream deferred" is from the Langston Hughes poem "Harlem" (Hughes, *Collected Poems*, [New York: Random House, 1990]). The phrase is also closely associated with the Lorraine Hansbury play, *A Raisin in the Sun*, which uses Langston's poem as epigraph and theme. See https://www.poetryfoundation.org/poems/46548/harlem.

3. "What is Aldersgate Day?" The United Methodist Church, www.umc.org /what-we-believe/what-is-aldersgate-day.

4. Mari Evans, "Celebration," in *A Dark and Splendid Mass* (New York: Harlem River Press, 1992). Used with permission.

June

1. Written by Rev. Beth Rauen Sciaino, 2010. Included with permission.

July

1. Mark A. Miller and Laurie Zelman, "Sower Song," in *Amazing Abundance* by Mark Miller (Nashville: Abingdon Press, 2003).

September

1. "Wave Motion," FuseSchool, December 19, 2017, www.youtube.com /watch?v=CVsdXKO9xlk.

October

1. Frederick Buechner, *Wishful Thinking* (London: Mowbray, 1994).

2. Suzanne Simard, "How Trees Talk to Each Other," TED Talk, August 30, 2016, www.youtube.com/watch?v=Un2yBgIAxYs.

November

1. Mary Oliver, "The Summer Day," in *New and Selected Poems* (Boston: Beacon, 1992).

Essay: "A Case for Homiletic Empathy"—Lenny Luchetti

1. Derek Matravers, "Empathy as a Route to Knowledge," in *Empathy: Philosophical and Psychological Perspectives*, eds. Amy Coplan and Peter Goldie (Oxford: Oxford University Press, 2011), 19.

2. Amy Coplan and Peter Goldie, "Introduction," in *Empathy: Philosophical and Psychological Perspectives*, (Oxford: Oxford University Press, 2011), xxi.

3. Alvin I. Goldman, "Two Routes to Empathy: Insights from Cognitive Neuroscience," in *Empathy: Philosophical and Psychological Perspectives*, 32.

4. Roman Krznaric, *Empathy: Why it Matters and How to Get It* (New York: Perigree, 2014), x.

Essay: "Preaching to Millennials"—Charley Reeb

1. Michael Duduit, blog ed. "3 Tips for Preaching to Millennials by Charley Reeb," preaching.com, https://www.preaching.com/articles/3-tips-for-preaching-to-millenials/. Adapted with permission.

Essay: "Soul Wounds in the Church"—Joni S. Sancken

1. Carolyn Yoder, *The Little Book of Trauma Healing* (Intercourse, PA: Good, 2005), 52–53; Marie Fortune, *Sexual Violence: The Sin Revisited* (Pasadena, TX: Pilgrim, 2005), 186–87.

2. Hillary Jerome Scarsella, "Responding to Reports of Abuse: Who's Getting It Right? And Where Does Theology Come In?" January 26, 2018, http://www.ourstoriesuntold.com/responding-to-reports-of-abuse/.

Essay: "Modern and Internet Ages: The Social Context of Preaching"—Paul Scott Wilson

1. James K. A. Smith, *Who's Afraid of Postmodernism? Taking Derrida, Lyotard, and Foucault to Church* (Grand Rapids: Baker Academic, 2006).

2. Paul Scott Wilson, *Preaching as Poetry: Beauty, Goodness, and Truth in Every Sermon* (Nashville: Abingdon Press, 2014).

3. One example of postmodern thought in homiletics is Jacob D. Myers, "Troubling Homiletics: Why Preaching Must Die," The Academy of Homiletics Workgroup Papers, 2017 (Academy of Homiletics, http://homiletics.org/). It is based on his *Preaching Must Die! Troubling Homiletical Theology* (Minneapolis, MN: Fortress, 2017). He says: "Homiletics exists to free preaching from theology. Homiletics is neither words about God nor God's 'Word,' *if* there is such a *thing*. Homiletics, like theology, like preaching, can have no life in and of itself. I believe that homiletics' sole purpose is to help preaching die a good death" (54). His comments have a certain philosophical value, and his paper seems to be based on a deep faith. His comments also suggest loyalty to the academy's need for innovation at the expense of Christian heritage, the faith needs of the local church, and the realities of struggling pastors in daily ministry.

4. See my discussion of this in *Preaching as Poetry*, 125–37.

Contributors

Lectionary Sermon and Worship Helps

Sheila Beckford—senior pastor, Wethersfield UMC, Wethersfield, CT
May 24; December 6

Tanya Linn Bennett—general editor, *The Abingdon Preaching Annual 2020;* associate dean for vocation and formation, and professor in the practice of public theology and vocation, Drew University Theological School, Madison, NJ; ordained elder, Greater New Jersey Conference, UMC
January 5; February 23; May 31; September 27; November 8

Susan Henry Crowe—general secretary, General Board of Church and Society, UMC; former dean of the chapel and religious life, Emory University, Atlanta, GA
December 20

Sudarshana Devadhar—resident bishop, Boston Area, UMC
April 5; August 2; December 13

Drew Dyson—ordained United Methodist elder; executive director, Princeton Senior Resource Center; Princeton, NJ
March 29; August 23

LaTrelle Easterling—resident bishop, and first woman to lead the historic Baltimore–Washington Conference, UMC
March 1; July 5; December 24

Heather Murray Elkins—professor of worship, preaching, and the arts, Drew University Theological School, Madison, NJ
March 8; July 26; November 15

Vicki Flippin—lead pastor, First and Summerfield UMC, New Haven, CT
April 10; September 6; October 25

Alisha Gordon—scholar activist; executive for spiritual growth, United Methodist Women, New York, NY
May 31; June 14; December 25

Grant Hagiya—resident bishop, Los Angeles Area, California-Pacific Conference, UMC
February 9; June 21; September 20

Christopher Heckert—senior pastor, Haddonfield UMC, Haddonfield, NJ
April 19; November 29

James McIntire—lead pastor, Royersford UMC, Royersford, PA
April 9; October 11

Mark A. Miller—associate professor of church music, director of the chapel, composer-in-residence, Drew University Theological School, Madison, NJ; lecturer in sacred music, Institute of Sacred Music, Yale Divinity School
January 19; April 12

Lydia Muñoz—worship designer; lead pastor, Church of the Open Door, Kennett Square, PA
March 15; October 4

Harriett Olson—chief executive officer, policymaking, United Methodist Women, New York, NY; graduate of Harvard Law School
February 26; May 31

Grace Pak—director of cross-racial / cross-cultural leadership, General Commission on Religion and Race, UMC
February 16; July 19; November 26

Jennifer Pick—liturgical worship specialist and pastor at First UMC, Mexia, TX; Central Texas Conference, UMC
May 17; August 16; October 18; December 27

Todd Pick—liturgical artist and graphic designer; pastor, Wesley Chapel–Gholson, Central Texas Conference, UMC
May 17; August 16; October 18; December 27

Gary Simpson—associate professor of homiletics, Drew University Theological School; senior pastor, Concord Baptist Church of Christ, Brooklyn, NY
January 26; June 7; November 22

Kathleen Stone—senior pastor, Wharton United Community Church at St. John's, a UMC and Presbyterian Church (U.S.A.) congregation, Wharton, NJ
March 22; August 9

J. Terry Todd—associate professor of American religious studies, Drew University Theological School, Madison, NJ; ordained pastor, Fellowship of Affirming Ministries
May 10; November 1

Javier Viera—vice provost, dean, professor of pastoral theology, Drew University Theological School, Madison, NJ
January 12; May 3

Jim Winkler—president and general secretary, National Council of Churches, Washington, DC
April 26; August 30

Karyn L. Wiseman—associate professor of homiletics, United Lutheran Seminary, Philadelphia, PA; pastor, Gloria Dei Church, Huntington Valley, PA
February 2; June 28

Laurie Zelman—published lyricist; mental health counselor; NewBridge Services; ordained deacon at Montville UMC, NJ
March 29; July 12; September 13

Contributors
Essays for Skill-Building

Lenny Luchetti is professor of proclamation and Christian Ministry at Wesley Seminary, Indiana Wesleyan University in Marion, Indiana. He is the author of *Preaching with Empathy: Crafting Sermons in a Callous Culture* in The Artistry of Preaching Series (Abingdon Press, 2018).

Charley Reeb is senior pastor of Johns Creek United Methodist Church just north of Atlanta, Georgia. He has served as a pastor for nearly twenty-five years in churches of every size. Under his preaching-focused leadership, each of those congregations has seen significant—sometimes extraordinary—growth. Charley's passion is helping other preachers, and he speaks and teaches nationally on the topic. He is the author of *That'll Preach! 5 Simple Steps to Your Best Sermon Ever* (Abingdon Press, 2017) and *Say Something! Simple Ways to Make Your Sermons Matter* (Abingdon Press, 2019).

Joni S. Sancken is associate professor of homiletics at United Theological Seminary in Dayton, Ohio. She is interested in theological and contextual issues in preaching and is the author of *Words That Heal: Preaching Hope to Wounded Souls* in The Artistry of Preaching Series (Abingdon Press, 2019). Joni is an ordained pastor in the Mennonite Church USA, served congregations in Indiana and Pennsylvania, and completed level-one STAR (Strategies for Trauma Awareness and Resilience) training through the Center for Justice and Peacebuilding at Eastern Mennonite University in 2017.

David B. Ward is associate professor of homiletics and practical theology at Indiana Wesleyan University in Marion, Indiana. He is an ordained minister in the Wesleyan Church who has served in a variety of roles including part-time pastor, full-time pastor, itinerant preacher, preaching professor, and academic dean. He is the author of *Practicing the Preaching Life* (Abingdon Press, 2019).

Paul Scott Wilson is professor of homiletics at Emmanuel College of Victoria University in the University of Toronto in Ontario. Canada. He is the author of *The Four Pages of the Sermon, Revised and Updated: A Guide to Biblical Preaching* (Abingdon Press, 2018) and the editor of Abingdon's The Artistry of Preaching Series.

Scripture Index

Online Edition

The Abingdon Preaching Annual 2020
online edition is available by subscription at
www.ministrymatters.com.

Abingdon Press is pleased to make available an online edition of *The Abingdon Preaching Annual 2020* as part of our Ministry Matters online community and resources.

Subscribers to our online edition will also have access to preaching content from prior years.

Visit www.ministrymatters.com and click on SUBSCRIBE NOW. From that menu, select "Abingdon Preaching Annual" and follow the prompt to set up an account.

If you have logged into an existing Ministry Matters account, you can subscribe to any of our online resources by simply clicking on MORE SUBSCRIPTIONS and following the prompts.

Please note, your subscription to *The Abingdon Preaching Annual* will be renewed automatically, unless you contact MinistryMatters.com to request a change.